# THE ANGEL
# AND THE AUTHOR—
# AND OTHERS

## Jerome K. Jerome

1st WORLD
LIBRARY
Literary Society

# The Angel and the Author - and others

## Jerome K. Jerome

© 1st World Library, 2007
PO Box 2211
Fairfield, IA 52556
www.1stworldlibrary.com
First Edition

LCCN: 2007920668

Softcover ISBN: 978-1-4218-3980-6
Hardcover ISBN: 978-1-4218-3880-9
eBook ISBN: 978-1-4218-4080-2

Purchase *"The Angel and the Author - and others"*
as a traditional bound book at:
www.1stWorldLibrary.com/purchase.asp?ISBN=978-1-4218-3980-6

1st World Library is a literary, educational organization
dedicated to:

- Creating a free internet library of downloadable ebooks

- Hosting writing competitions and offering book
  publishing scholarships.

# 1$^{st}$ World Library Literary Society

## Giving Back to the World

"If you want to work on the core problem, it's early school literacy."

**- James Barksdale, former CEO of Netscape**

"No skill is more crucial to the future of a child, or to a democratic and prosperous society, than literacy."

**- Los Angeles Times**

Literacy... means far more than learning how to read and write... The aim is to transmit... knowledge and promote social participation."

**- UNESCO**

"Literacy is not a luxury, it is a right and a responsibility. If our world is to meet the challenges of the twenty-first century we must harness the energy and creativity of all our citizens."

**- President Bill Clinton**

"Parents should be encouraged to read to their children, and teachers should be equipped with all available techniques for teaching literacy, so the varying needs and capacities of individual kids can be taken into account."

**- Hugh Mackay**

# CHAPTER I

I had a vexing dream one night, not long ago: it was about a fortnight after Christmas. I dreamt I flew out of the window in my nightshirt. I went up and up. I was glad that I was going up. "They have been noticing me," I thought to myself. "If anything, I have been a bit too good. A little less virtue and I might have lived longer. But one cannot have everything." The world grew smaller and smaller. The last I saw of London was the long line of electric lamps bordering the Embankment; later nothing remained but a faint luminosity buried beneath darkness. It was at this point of my journey that I heard behind me the slow, throbbing sound of wings.

I turned my head. It was the Recording Angel. He had a weary look; I judged him to be tired.

"Yes," he acknowledged, "it is a trying period for me, your Christmas time."

"I am sure it must be," I returned; "the wonder to me is how you get through it all. You see at Christmas time," I went on, "all we men and women become generous, quite suddenly. It is really a delightful sensation."

"You are to be envied," he agreed.

"It is the first Christmas number that starts me off," I told him; "those beautiful pictures—the sweet child looking so pretty in her furs, giving Bovril with her own dear little hands to the shivering street arab; the good old red-faced squire shovelling out plum pudding to the crowd of grateful villagers. It makes me yearn to borrow a collecting box and go round doing good myself.

"And it is not only me—I should say I," I continued; "I don't want you to run away with the idea that I am the only good man in the world. That's what I like about Christmas, it makes everybody good. The lovely sentiments we go about repeating! the noble deeds we do! from a little before Christmas up to, say, the end of January! why noting them down must be a comfort to you."

"Yes," he admitted, "noble deeds are always a great joy to me."

"They are to all of us," I said; "I love to think of all the good deeds I myself have done. I have often thought of keeping a diary—jotting them down each day. It would be so nice for one's children."

He agreed there was an idea in this.

"That book of yours," I said, "I suppose, now, it contains all the good actions that we men and women have been doing during the last six weeks?" It was a bulky looking volume.

Yes, he answered, they were all recorded in the book.

[The Author tells of his Good Deeds.]

It was more for the sake of talking of his than anything else that I kept up with him. I did not really doubt his care and conscientiousness, but it is always pleasant to chat about one's self. "My five shillings subscription to the Daily Telegraph's Sixpenny Fund for the Unemployed—got that down all right?" I asked him.

Yes, he replied, it was entered.

"As a matter of fact, now I come to think of it," I added, "it was ten shillings altogether. They spelt my name wrong the first time."

Both subscriptions had been entered, he told me.

"Then I have been to four charity dinners," I reminded him; "I forget what the particular charity was about. I know I suffered the next morning. Champagne never does agree with me. But, then, if you don't order it people think you can't afford it. Not that I don't like it. It's my liver, if you understand. If I take more—"

He interrupted me with the assurance that my attendance had been noted.

"Last week I sent a dozen photographs of myself, signed, to a charity bazaar."

He said he remembered my doing so.

"Then let me see," I continued, "I have been to two ordinary balls. I don't care much about dancing, but a few of us generally play a little bridge; and to one fancy dress affair. I went as Sir Walter Raleigh. Some men cannot afford to show their leg. What I say is, if a man can, why not? It isn't often that one gets the opportunity of really looking one's best."

He told me all three balls had been duly entered: and commented upon.

"And, of course, you remember my performance of Talbot Champneys in Our Boys the week before last, in aid of the Fund for Poor Curates," I went on. "I don't know whether you saw the notice in the Morning Post, but—"

He again interrupted me to remark that what the Morning Post man said would be entered, one way or the other, to the critic of the Morning Post, and had nothing to do with me.

"Of course not," I agreed; "and between ourselves, I don't think the charity got very much. Expenses, when you come to add refreshments and one thing and another, mount up. But I fancy they rather liked my Talbot Champneys."

He replied that he had been present at the performance, and had made his own report.

I also reminded him of the four balcony seats I had taken for the monster show at His Majesty's in aid of the Fund for the Destitute British in Johannesburg. Not all the celebrated actors and actresses announced on the posters had appeared, but all had sent letters full of kindly wishes; and the others—all the celebrities one had never heard of—had turned up to a man. Still, on the whole, the show was well worth the money. There was nothing to grumble at.

There were other noble deeds of mine. I could not remember them at the time in their entirety. I seemed to have done a good many. But I did remember the rummage sale to which I sent all my old clothes, including a coat that had got mixed up with them by accident, and that I believe I could have worn again.

And also the raffle I had joined for a motor-car.

The Angel said I really need not be alarmed, that everything had been noted, together with other matters I, may be, had forgotten.

[The Angel appears to have made a slight Mistake.]

I felt a certain curiosity. We had been getting on very well together—so it had seemed to me. I asked him if he would mind my seeing the book. He said there could be no objection. He opened it at the page devoted to myself, and I flew a little higher, and looked down over his shoulder. I can hardly believe it, even now—that I could have dreamt anything so foolish:

Jerome K. Jerome

He had got it all down wrong!

Instead of to the credit side of my account he had put the whole bag of tricks to my debit. He had mixed them up with my sins—with my acts of hypocrisy, vanity, self-indulgence. Under the head of Charity he had but one item to my credit for the past six months: my giving up my seat inside a tramcar, late one wet night, to a dismal- looking old woman, who had not had even the politeness to say "thank you," she seemed just half asleep. According to this idiot, all the time and money I had spent responding to these charitable appeals had been wasted.

I was not angry with him, at first. I was willing to regard what he had done as merely a clerical error.

"You have got the items down all right," I said (I spoke quite friendly), "but you have made a slight mistake—we all do now and again; you have put them down on the wrong side of the book. I only hope this sort of thing doesn't occur often."

What irritated me as much as anything was the grave, passionless face the Angel turned upon me.

"There is no mistake," he answered.

"No mistake!" I cried. "Why, you blundering—"

He closed the book with a weary sigh.

I felt so mad with him, I went to snatch it out of his hand. He did not do anything that I was aware of, but at once I began falling. The faint luminosity beneath me grew, and then the lights of London seemed shooting up to meet me. I was coming down on the clock tower at Westminster. I gave myself a convulsive twist, hoping to escape it, and fell into the river.

And then I awoke.

But it stays with me: the weary sadness of the Angel's face. I cannot shake remembrance from me. Would I have done better, had I taken the money I had spent upon these fooleries, gone down with it among the poor myself, asking nothing in return. Is this fraction of our superfluity, flung without further thought or care into the collection box, likely to satisfy the Impracticable Idealist, who actually suggested—one shrugs one's shoulders when one thinks of it—that one should sell all one had and give to the poor?

[The Author is troubled concerning his Investments.]

Or is our charity but a salve to conscience—an insurance, at decidedly moderate premium, in case, after all, there should happen to be another world? Is Charity lending to the Lord something we can so easily do without?

I remember a lady tidying up her house, clearing it of rubbish. She called it "Giving to the Fresh Air Fund." Into the heap of lumber one of her daughters flung a pair of crutches that for years had been knocking about the house. The lady picked them out again.

"We won't give those away," she said, "they might come in useful again. One never knows."

Another lady, I remember coming downstairs one evening dressed for a fancy ball. I forget the title of the charity, but I remember that every lady who sold more than ten tickets received an autograph letter of thanks from the Duchess who was the president. The tickets were twelve and sixpence each and included light refreshments and a very substantial supper. One presumes the odd sixpence reached the poor—or at least the noisier portion of them.

"A little decolletee, isn't it, my dear?" suggested a lady friend, as the charitable dancer entered the drawing-room.

"Perhaps it is—a little," she admitted, "but we all of us ought

　　　　Jerome K. Jerome

to do all we can for the Cause. Don't you think so, dear?"

Really, seeing the amount we give in charity, the wonder is there are any poor left. It is a comfort that there are. What should we do without them? Our fur-clad little girls! our jolly, red-faced squires! we should never know how good they were, but for the poor? Without the poor how could we be virtuous? We should have to go about giving to each other. And friends expect such expensive presents, while a shilling here and there among the poor brings to us all the sensations of a good Samaritan. Providence has been very thoughtful in providing us with poor.

Dear Lady Bountiful! does it not ever occur to you to thank God for the poor? The clean, grateful poor, who bob their heads and curtsey and assure you that heaven is going to repay you a thousandfold. One does hope you will not be disappointed.

An East-End curate once told me, with a twinkle in his eye, of a smart lady who called upon him in her carriage, and insisted on his going round with her to show her where the poor hid themselves. They went down many streets, and the lady distributed her parcels. Then they came to one of the worst, a very narrow street. The coachman gave it one glance.

"Sorry, my lady," said the coachman, "but the carriage won't go down."

The lady sighed.

"I am afraid we shall have to leave it," she said.

So the gallant greys dashed past.

Where the real poor creep I fear there is no room for Lady Bountiful's fine coach. The ways are very narrow—wide enough only for little Sister Pity, stealing softly.

I put it to my friend, the curate:

"But if all this charity is, as you say, so useless; if it touches but the fringe; if it makes the evil worse, what would you do?"

[And questions a Man of Thought]

"I would substitute Justice," he answered; "there would be no need for Charity."

"But it is so delightful to give," I answered.

"Yes," he agreed. "It is better to give than to receive. I was thinking of the receiver. And my ideal is a long way off. We shall have to work towards it slowly."

# CHAPTER II

[Philosophy and the Daemon]

Philosophy, it has been said, is the art of bearing other people's troubles. The truest philosopher I ever heard of was a woman. She was brought into the London Hospital suffering from a poisoned leg. The house surgeon made a hurried examination. He was a man of blunt speech.

"It will have to come off," he told her.

"What, not all of it?"

"The whole of it, I am sorry to say," growled the house surgeon.

"Nothing else for it?"

"No other chance for you whatever," explained the house surgeon.

"Ah, well, thank Gawd it's not my 'ead," observed the lady.

The poor have a great advantage over us better-off folk. Providence provides them with many opportunities for the practice of philosophy. I was present at a "high tea" given last winter by charitable folk to a party of char-women. After the tables were cleared we sought to amuse them. One young lady, who was proud of herself as a palmist, set out to study their "lines." At sight of the first toil-worn hand she took hold of her sympathetic face grew sad.

"There is a great trouble coming to you," she informed the ancient dame.

The placid-featured dame looked up and smiled:

"What, only one, my dear?"

"Yes, only one," asserted the kind fortune-teller, much pleased, "after that all goes smoothly."

"Ah," murmured the old dame, quite cheerfully, "we was all of us a short-lived family."

Our skins harden to the blows of Fate. I was lunching one Wednesday with a friend in the country. His son and heir, aged twelve, entered and took his seat at the table.

"Well," said his father, "and how did we get on at school today?"

"Oh, all right," answered the youngster, settling himself down to his dinner with evident appetite.

"Nobody caned?" demanded his father, with—as I noticed—a sly twinkle in his eye.

"No," replied young hopeful, after reflection; "no, I don't think so," adding as an afterthought, as he tucked into beef and potatoes, "'cepting, o' course, me."

[When the Daemon will not work]

It is a simple science, philosophy. The idea is that it never matters what happens to you provided you don't mind it. The weak point in the argument is that nine times out of ten you can't help minding it.

Jerome K. Jerome

"No misfortune can harm me," says Marcus Aurelius, "without the consent of the daemon within me."

The trouble is our daemon cannot always be relied upon. So often he does not seem up to his work.

"You've been a naughty boy, and I'm going to whip you," said nurse to a four-year-old criminal.

"You tant," retorted the young ruffian, gripping with both hands the chair that he was occupying, "I'se sittin' on it."

His daemon was, no doubt, resolved that misfortune, as personified by nurse, should not hurt him. The misfortune, alas! proved stronger than the daemon, and misfortune, he found did hurt him.

The toothache cannot hurt us so long as the daemon within us (that is to say, our will power) holds on to the chair and says it can't. But, sooner or later, the daemon lets go, and then we howl. One sees the idea: in theory it is excellent. One makes believe. Your bank has suddenly stopped payment. You say to yourself.

"This does not really matter."

Your butcher and your baker say it does, and insist on making a row in the passage.

You fill yourself up with gooseberry wine. You tell yourself it is seasoned champagne. Your liver next morning says it is not.

The daemon within us means well, but forgets it is not the only thing there. A man I knew was an enthusiast on vegetarianism. He argued that if the poor would adopt a vegetarian diet the problem of existence would be simpler for them, and maybe he was right. So one day he assembled some twenty poor lads for the purpose of introducing to them a vegetarian lunch. He begged them to believe that lentil beans were steaks, that cauliflowers were chops. As a third course he placed before them a mixture of carrots and savoury herbs, and urged them to imagine they were eating saveloys.

"Now, you all like saveloys," he said, addressing them, "and the palate is but the creature of the imagination. Say to yourselves, 'I am eating saveloys,' and for all practical purposes these things will be saveloys."

Some of the lads professed to have done it, but one disappointed- looking youth confessed to failure.

"But how can you be sure it was not a saveloy?" the host persisted.

"Because," explained the boy, "I haven't got the stomach-ache."

It appeared that saveloys, although a dish of which he was fond, invariably and immediately disagreed with him. If only we were all daemon and nothing else philosophy would be easier. Unfortunately, there is more of us.

Another argument much approved by philosophy is that nothing matters, because a hundred years hence, say, at the outside, we shall be dead. What we really want is a philosophy that will enable us to get along while we are still alive. I am not worrying about my centenary; I am worrying about next quarter-day. I feel that if other people would only go away, and leave me—income-tax collectors, critics, men who come round about the gas, all those sort of people—I could be a philosopher myself. I am willing enough to make believe that nothing matters, but they are not. They say it is going to be cut off, and talk about judgment summonses. I tell them it won't trouble any of us a hundred years hence. They answer they are not talking of a hundred years hence, but of this thing that was due last April twelvemonth. They won't listen to my daemon. He does not interest them. Nor, to be candid, does it comfort myself very much, this philosophical reflection that a hundred years later on I'll be sure to be dead—that is, with ordinary luck. What bucks me up much more is the hope that they will be dead. Besides, in a hundred years things may have improved. I may not want to be dead. If I were sure of being dead next morning, before their threat of cutting off that water or that gas could by any possibility be carried out, before that judgment summons they are bragging about could be made returnable, I might—I don't say I should—be amused, thinking how I was going to dish them. The wife of a very wicked man visited him one evening in prison, and found him enjoying a supper of toasted cheese.

"How foolish of you, Edward," argued the fond lady, "to be eating toasted cheese for supper. You know it always affects your liver. All day long to-morrow you will be complaining."

"No, I shan't," interrupted Edward; "not so foolish as you think me. They are going to hang me to-morrow—early."

There is a passage in Marcus Aurelius that used to puzzle me until I hit upon the solution. A foot-note says the meaning is obscure. Myself, I had gathered this before I read the foot-note. What it is all about I defy any human being to explain. It might mean anything; it might mean nothing. The majority of students incline to the latter theory, though a minority maintain there is a meaning, if only it could be discovered. My own conviction is that once in his life Marcus Aurelius had a real good time. He came home feeling pleased with himself without knowing quite why.

"I will write it down," he said to himself, "now, while it is fresh in my mind."

It seemed to him the most wonderful thing that anybody had ever said. Maybe he shed a tear or two, thinking of all the good he was doing, and later on went suddenly to sleep. In the morning he had forgotten all about it, and by accident it got mixed up with the rest of the book. That is the only explanation that seems to me possible, and it comforts me.

We are none of us philosophers all the time.

Philosophy is the science of suffering the inevitable, which most of us contrive to accomplish without the aid of philosophy. Marcus Aurelius was an Emperor of Rome, and Diogenes was a bachelor living rent free. I want the philosophy of the bank clerk married on thirty shillings a week, of the farm labourer bringing up a family of eight on a precarious wage of twelve shillings. The troubles of Marcus Aurelius were chiefly those of other people.

"Taxes will have to go up, I am afraid," no doubt he often sighed. "But, after all, what are taxes? A thing in conformity with the nature of man—a little thing that Zeus approves of, one feels sure. The daemon within me says taxes don't really matter."

Maybe the paterfamilias of the period, who did the paying, worried about new sandals for the children, his wife insisting she hadn't a frock fit to be seen in at the amphitheatre; that, if there was one thing in the world she fancied, it was seeing a Christian eaten by a lion, but now she supposed the children would have to go without her, found that philosophy came to his aid less readily.

"Bother these barbarians," Marcus Aurelius may have been tempted, in an unphilosophical moment, to exclaim; "I do wish they would not burn these poor people's houses over their heads, toss the babies about on spears, and carry off the older children into slavery. Why don't they behave themselves?"

But philosophy in Marcus Aurelius would eventually triumph over passing fretfulness.

"But how foolish of me to be angry with them," he would argue with himself. "One is not vexed with the fig-tree for yielding figs, with the cucumber for being bitter! One must expect barbarians to behave barbariously."

Jerome K. Jerome

Marcus Aurelius would proceed to slaughter the barbarians, and then forgive them. We can most of us forgive our brother his transgressions, having once got even with him. In a tiny Swiss village, behind the angle of the school-house wall, I came across a maiden crying bitterly, her head resting on her arm. I asked her what had happened. Between her sobs she explained that a school companion, a little lad about her own age, having snatched her hat from her head, was at that moment playing football with it the other side of the wall. I attempted to console her with philosophy. I pointed out to her that boys would be boys—that to expect from them at that age reverence for feminine headgear was to seek what was not conformable with the nature of boy. But she appeared to have no philosophy in her. She said he was a horrid boy, and that she hated him. It transpired it was a hat she rather fancied herself in. He peeped round the corner while we were talking, the hat in his hand. He held it out to her, but she took no notice of him. I gathered the incident was closed, and went my way, but turned a few steps further on, curious to witness the end. Step by step he approached nearer, looking a little ashamed of himself; but still she wept, her face hidden in her arm.

He was not expecting it: to all seeming she stood there the personification of the grief that is not to be comforted, oblivious to all surroundings. Incautiously he took another step. In an instant she had "landed" him over the head with a long narrow wooden box containing, one supposes, pencils and pens. He must have been a hard-headed youngster, the sound of the compact echoed through the valley. I met her again on my way back.

"Hat much damaged?" I inquired.

"Oh, no," she answered, smiling; "besides, it was only an old hat. I've got a better one for Sundays."

I often feel philosophical myself; generally over a good cigar after a satisfactory dinner. At such times I open my Marcus Aurelius, my pocket Epicurus, my translation of Plato's

"Republic." At such times I agree with them. Man troubles himself too much about the unessential. Let us cultivate serenity. Nothing can happen to us that we have not been constituted by Nature to sustain. That foolish farm labourer, on his precarious wage of twelve shillings a week: let him dwell rather on the mercies he enjoys. Is he not spared all anxiety concerning safe investment of capital yielding four per cent.? Is not the sunrise and the sunset for him also? Many of us never see the sunrise. So many of our so-termed poorer brethen are privileged rarely to miss that early morning festival. Let the daemon within them rejoice. Why should he fret when the children cry for bread? Is it not in the nature of things that the children of the poor should cry for bread? The gods in their wisdom have arranged it thus. Let the daemon within him reflect upon the advantage to the community of cheap labour. Let the farm labourer contemplate the universal good.

# CHAPTER III

[Literature and the Middle Classes.]

I am sorry to be compelled to cast a slur upon the Literary profession, but observation shows me that it still contains within its ranks writers born and bred in, and moving amidst—if, without offence, one may put it bluntly—a purely middle-class environment: men and women to whom Park Lane will never be anything than the shortest route between Notting Hill and the Strand; to whom Debrett's Peerage—gilt-edged and bound in red, a tasteful-looking volume—ever has been and ever will remain a drawing-room ornament and not a social necessity. Now what is to become of these writers—of us, if for the moment I may be allowed to speak as representative of this rapidly-diminishing yet nevertheless still numerous section of the world of Art and Letters? Formerly, provided we were masters of style, possessed imagination and insight, understood human nature, had sympathy with and knowledge of life, and could express ourselves with humour and distinction, our pathway was, comparatively speaking, free from obstacle. We drew from the middle-class life around us, passed it through our own middle-class individuality, and presented it to a public composed of middle-class readers.

But the middle-class public, for purposes of Art, has practically disappeared. The social strata from which George Eliot and Dickens drew their characters no longer interests the great B. P. Hetty Sorrell, Little Em'ly, would be pronounced "provincial;" a Deronda or a Wilfer Family ignored as "suburban."

I confess that personally the terms "provincial" and "suburban," as epithets of reproach, have always puzzled me. I never met anyone more severe on what she termed the "suburban note" in literature than a thin lady who lived in a semi-detached villa in a by-street of Hammersmith. Is Art merely a question of geography, and if so what is the exact limit? Is it the four-mile cab radius from Charing Cross? Is the cheesemonger of Tottenham Court Road of necessity a man of taste, and the Oxford professor of necessity a Philistine? I want to understand this thing. I once hazarded the direct question to a critical friend:

"You say a book is suburban," I put it to him, "and there is an end to the matter. But what do you mean by suburban?"

"Well," he replied, "I mean it is the sort of book likely to appeal to the class that inhabits the suburbs." He lived himself in Chancery Lane.

[May a man of intelligence live, say, in Surbiton?]

"But there is Jones, the editor of The Evening Gentleman," I argued; "he lives at Surbiton. It is just twelve miles from Waterloo. He comes up every morning by the eight-fifteen and returns again by the five-ten. Would you say that a book is bound to be bad because it appeals to Jones? Then again, take Tomlinson: he lives, as you are well aware, at Forest Gate which is Epping way, and entertains you on Kakemonos whenever you call upon him. You know what I mean, of course. I think 'Kakemono' is right. They are long things; they look like coloured hieroglyphics printed on brown paper. He gets behind them and holds them up above his head on the end of a stick so that you can see the whole of them at once; and he tells you the name of the Japanese artist who painted them in the year 1500 B.C., and what it is all about. He shows them to you by the hour and forgets to give you dinner. There isn't an easy chair in the house. To put it vulgarly, what is wrong with Tomlinson from a high art point of view?

"There's a man I know who lives in Birmingham: you must have heard of him. He is the great collector of Eighteenth Century caricatures, the Rowlandson and Gilray school of things. I don't call them artistic myself; they make me ill to look at them; but people who understand Art rave about them. Why can't a man be artistic who has got a cottage in the country?"

"You don't understand me," retorted my critical friend, a little irritably, as I thought.

"I admit it," I returned. "It is what I am trying to do."

"Of course artistic people live in the suburbs," he admitted. "But they are not of the suburbs."

"Though they may dwell in Wimbledon or Hornsey," I suggested, "they sing with the Scotch bard: 'My heart is in the South-West postal district. My heart is not here.'"

"You can put it that way if you like," he growled.

"I will, if you have no objection," I agreed. "It makes life easier for those of us with limited incomes."

The modern novel takes care, however, to avoid all doubt upon the subject. Its personages, one and all, reside within the half-mile square lying between Bond Street and the Park—a neighbourhood that would appear to be somewhat densely populated. True, a year or two ago there appeared a fairly successful novel the heroine of which resided in Onslow Gardens. An eminent critic observed of it that: "It fell short only by a little way of being a serious contribution to English literature." Consultation with the keeper of the cabman's shelter at Hyde Park Corner suggested to me that the "little way" the critic had in mind measures exactly eleven hundred yards. When the nobility and gentry of the modern novel do leave London they do not go into the provinces: to do that would be vulgar. They make straight for "Barchester Towers," or what the Duke calls "his little place up north"—localities, one presumes, suspended somewhere in mid-air.

In every social circle exist great souls with yearnings towards higher things. Even among the labouring classes one meets with naturally refined natures, gentlemanly persons to whom the loom and the plough will always appear low, whose natural desire is towards the dignities and graces of the servants' hall. So in Grub Street we can always reckon upon the superior writer whose temperament will prompt him to make respectful study of his betters. A reasonable supply of high-class novels might always have been depended upon; the trouble is that the public now demands that all stories must be of the upper ten thousand. Auld Robin Grey must be Sir Robert Grey, South African millionaire; and Jamie, the youngest son of the old Earl, otherwise a cultured public can take no interest in the ballad. A modern nursery rhymester to succeed would have to write of Little Lord Jack and Lady Jill ascending one of the many beautiful eminences belonging to the ancestral estates of their parents, bearing between them, on a silver rod, an exquisitely painted Sevres vase filled with ottar of roses.

I take up my fourpenny-halfpenny magazine. The heroine is a youthful Duchess; her husband gambles with thousand-pound notes, with the result that they are reduced to living on the first floor of the Carlton Hotel. The villain is a Russian Prince. The Baronet of a simpler age has been unable, poor fellow, to keep pace with the times. What self-respecting heroine would abandon her husband and children for sin and a paltry five thousand a year? To the heroine of the past—to the clergyman's daughter or the lady artist—he was dangerous. The modern heroine misbehaves herself with nothing below Cabinet rank.

I turn to something less pretentious, a weekly periodical that my wife tells me is the best authority she has come across on blouses. I find in it what once upon a time would have been called a farce. It is now a "drawing-room comedietta. All rights reserved." The dramatis personae consist of the Earl of Danbury, the Marquis of Rottenborough (with a past), and an American heiress—a character that nowadays takes with lovers of the simple the place formerly occupied by "Rose, the miller's daughter."

I sometimes wonder, is it such teaching as that of Carlyle and Tennyson that is responsible for this present tendency of literature? Carlyle impressed upon us that the only history worth consideration was the life of great men and women, and Tennyson that we "needs must love the highest." So literature, striving ever upward, ignores plain Romola for the Lady Ponsonby de Tompkins; the provincialisms of a Charlotte Bronte for what a certain critic, born before his time, would have called the "doin's of the hupper succles."

The British Drama has advanced by even greater bounds. It takes place now exclusively within castle walls, and—what Messrs. Lumley & Co.'s circular would describe as—"desirable town mansions, suitable for gentlemen of means." A living dramatist, who should know, tells us that drama does not occur in the back parlour. Dramatists have, it has been argued, occasionally found it there, but such may have been dramatists with eyes capable of seeing through clothes.

I once wrote a play which I read to a distinguished Manager. He said it was a most interesting play: they always say that. I waited, wondering to what other manager he would recommend me to take it. To my surprise he told me he would like it for himself—but with alterations.

"The whole thing wants lifting up," was his opinion. "Your hero is a barrister: my public take no interest in plain barristers. Make him the Solicitor General."

"But he's got to be amusing," I argued. "A Solicitor General is never amusing."

My Manager pondered for a moment. "Let him be Solicitor General for Ireland," he suggested.

I made a note of it.

"Your heroine," he continued, "is the daughter of a seaside lodging-house keeper. My public do not recognize seaside lodgings. Why not the daughter of an hotel proprietor? Even that will be risky, but we might venture it." An inspiration came to him. "Or better still, let the old man be the Managing Director of an hotel Trust: that would account for her clothes."

Unfortunately I put the thing aside for a few months, and when I was ready again the public taste had still further advanced. The doors of the British Drama were closed for the time being on all but members of the aristocracy, and I did not see my comic old man as a Marquis, which was the lowest title that just then one dared to offer to a low comedian.

Now how are we middle-class novelists and dramatists to continue to live? I am aware of the obvious retort, but to us it absolutely is necessary. We know only parlours: we call them drawing-rooms. At the bottom of our middle-class hearts we regard them fondly: the folding-doors thrown back, they make rather a fine apartment. The only drama that we know takes place in such rooms: the hero sitting in the gentleman's easy chair, of green repp: the heroine in the lady's ditto, without arms—the chair, I mean. The scornful glances, the bitter words of our middle-class world are hurled across these three-legged loo-tables, the wedding-cake ornament under its glass case playing the part of white ghost.

In these days, when "Imperial cement" is at a premium, who would dare suggest that the emotions of a parlour can by any possibility be the same as those exhibited in a salon furnished in the style of Louis Quatorze; that the tears of Bayswater can possibly be compared for saltness with the lachrymal fluid distilled from South Audley Street glands; that the laughter of

Clapham can be as catching as the cultured cackle of Curzon Street? But we, whose best clothes are exhibited only in parlours, what are we to do? How can we lay bare the souls of Duchesses, explain the heart-throbs of peers of the realm? Some of my friends who, being Conservative, attend Primrose "tourneys" (or is it "Courts of love"? I speak as an outsider. Something mediaeval, I know it is) do, it is true, occasionally converse with titled ladies. But the period for conversation is always limited owing to the impatience of the man behind; and I doubt if the interview is ever of much practical use to them, as conveying knowledge of the workings of the aristocratic mind. Those of us who are not Primrose Knights miss even this poor glimpse into the world above us. We know nothing, simply nothing, concerning the deeper feelings of the upper ten. Personally, I once received a letter from an Earl, but that was in connection with a dairy company of which his lordship was chairman, and spoke only of his lordship's views concerning milk and the advantages of the cash system. Of what I really wished to know—his lordship's passions, yearnings and general attitude to life—the circular said nothing.

Year by year I find myself more and more in a minority. One by one my literary friends enter into this charmed aristocratic circle; after which one hears no more from them regarding the middle-classes. At once they set to work to describe the mental sufferings of Grooms of the Bed-chamber, the hidden emotions of Ladies in their own right, the religious doubts of Marquises. I want to know how they do it—"how the devil they get there." They refuse to tell me.

Meanwhile, I see nothing before me but the workhouse. Year by year the public grows more impatient of literature dealing merely with the middle-classes. I know nothing about any other class. What am I to do?

Commonplace people—friends of mine without conscience, counsel me in flippant phrase to "have a shot at it."

"I expect, old fellow, you know just as much about it as these other Johnnies do." (I am not defending their conversation either as regards style or matter: I am merely quoting.) "And even if you don't, what does it matter? The average reader knows less. How is he to find you out?"

But, as I explain to them, it is the law of literature never to write except about what you really know. I want to mix with the aristocracy, study them, understand them; so that I may earn my living in the only way a literary man nowadays can earn his living, namely, by writing about the upper circles.

I want to know how to get there.

# CHAPTER IV

[Man and his Master.]

There is one thing that the Anglo-Saxon does better than the "French, or Turk, or Rooshian," to which add the German or the Belgian. When the Anglo-Saxon appoints an official, he appoints a servant: when the others put a man in uniform, they add to their long list of masters. If among your acquaintances you can discover an American, or Englishman, unfamiliar with the continental official, it is worth your while to accompany him, the first time he goes out to post a letter, say. He advances towards the post-office a breezy, self-confident gentleman, borne up by pride of race. While mounting the steps he talks airily of "just getting this letter off his mind, and then picking up Jobson and going on to Durand's for lunch."

He talks as if he had the whole day before him. At the top of the steps he attempts to push open the door. It will not move. He looks about him, and discovers that is the door of egress, not of ingress. It does not seem to him worth while redescending the twenty steps and climbing another twenty. So far as he is concerned he is willing to pull the door, instead of pushing it. But a stern official bars his way, and haughtily indicates the proper entrance. "Oh, bother," he says, and down he trots again, and up the other flight.

"I shall not be a minute," he remarks over his shoulder. "You can wait for me outside."

But if you know your way about, you follow him in. There are seats within, and you have a newspaper in your pocket: the time will pass more pleasantly. Inside he looks round, bewildered. The German post-office, generally speaking, is about the size of the Bank of England. Some twenty different windows confront your troubled friend, each one bearing its own particular legend. Starting with number one, he sets to work to spell them out. It appears to him that the posting of letters is not a thing that the German post- office desires to encourage. Would he not like a dog licence instead? is what one window suggests to him. "Oh, never mind that letter of yours; come and talk about bicycles," pleads another. At last he thinks he has found the right hole: the word "Registration" he distinctly recognizes. He taps at the glass.

Nobody takes any notice of him. The foreign official is a man whose life is saddened by a public always wanting something. You read it in his face wherever you go. The man who sells you tickets for the theatre! He is eating sandwiches when you knock at his window. He turns to his companion:

"Good Lord!" you can see him say, "here's another of 'em. If there has been one man worrying me this morning there have been a hundred. Always the same story: all of 'em want to come and see the play. You listen now; bet you anything he's going to bother me for tickets. Really, it gets on my nerves sometimes."

At the railway station it is just the same.

"Another man who wants to go to Antwerp! Don't seem to care for rest, these people: flying here, flying there, what's the sense of it?" It is this absurd craze on the part of the public for letter-writing that is spoiling the temper of the continental post-office official. He does his best to discourage it.

"Look at them," he says to his assistant—the thoughtful German Government is careful to provide every official with another official for company, lest by sheer force of ennui he might be reduced to taking interest in his work—"twenty of 'em, all in a row! Some of 'em been there for the last quarter of an hour."

"Let 'em wait another quarter of an hour," advises the assistant; "perhaps they'll go away."

"My dear fellow," he answers, "do you think I haven't tried that? There's simply no getting rid of 'em. And it's always the same cry: 'Stamps! stamps! stamps!' 'Pon my word, I think they live on stamps, some of 'em."

"Well let 'em have their stamps?" suggests the assistant, with a burst of inspiration; "perhaps it will get rid of 'em."

[Why the Man in Uniform has, generally, sad Eyes.]

"What's the use?" wearily replies the older man. "There will only come a fresh crowd when those are gone."

"Oh, well," argues the other, "that will be a change, anyhow. I'm tired of looking at this lot."

I put it to a German post-office clerk once—a man I had been boring for months. I said:

"You think I write these letters—these short stories, these three-act plays—on purpose to annoy you. Do let me try to get the idea out of your head. Personally, I hate work—hate it as much as you do. This is a pleasant little town of yours: given a free choice, I could spend the whole day mooning round it, never putting pen to paper. But what am I to do? I have a wife and children. You know what it is yourself: they clamour for food, boots—all sorts of things. I have to prepare these little packets for sale and bring them to you to send off. You see, you are here. If you were not here—if there were no post-office in this town, maybe I'd have to train pigeons, or cork the thing up in a bottle, fling it into the river, and trust to luck and the Gulf Stream. But, you being here, and calling yourself a post-office—well, it's a temptation to a fellow."

I think it did good. Anyhow, after that he used to grin when I opened the door, instead of greeting me as formerly with a face the picture of despair. But to return to our inexperienced friend.

At last the wicket is suddenly opened. A peremptory official demands of him "name and address." Not expecting the question, he is a little doubtful of his address, and has to correct himself once or twice. The official eyes him suspiciously.

"Name of mother?" continues the official.

"Name of what?"

"Mother!" repeats the official. "Had a mother of some sort, I suppose."

He is a man who loved his mother sincerely while she lived, but she has been dead these twenty years, and, for the life of him he cannot recollect her name. He thinks it was Margaret Henrietta, but is not at all sure. Besides, what on earth has his mother got to do with this registered letter that he wants to send to his partner in New York?

"When did it die?" asks the official.

"When did what die? Mother?"

"No, no, the child."

"What child?" The indignation of the official is almost picturesque.

"All I want to do," explains your friend, "is to register a letter."

"A what?"

"This letter, I want—"

The window is slammed in his face. When, ten minutes later he does reach the right wicket—the bureau for the registration of letters, and not the bureau for the registration of infantile deaths—it is pointed out to him that the letter either is sealed or that it is not sealed.

I have never been able yet to solve this problem. If your letter is sealed, it then appears that it ought not to have been sealed.

If, on the other hand, you have omitted to seal it, that is your fault. In any case, the letter cannot go as it is. The continental official brings up the public on the principle of the nurse who sent the eldest girl to see what Tommy was doing and tell him he mustn't. Your friend, having wasted half an hour and mislaid his temper for the day, decides to leave this thing over and talk to the hotel porter about it. Next to the Burgomeister, the hotel porter is the most influential man in the continental town: maybe because he can swear in seven different languages. But even he is not omnipotent.

[The Traveller's one Friend.]

Three of us, on the point of starting for a walking tour through the Tyrol, once sent on our luggage by post from Constance to Innsbruck. Our idea was that, reaching Innsbruck in the height of the season, after a week's tramp on two flannel shirts and a change of socks, we should be glad to get into fresh clothes before showing ourselves in civilized society. Our bags were waiting for us in the post-office: we could see them through the grating. But some informality—I have never been able to understand what it was—had occurred at Constance. The suspicion of the Swiss postal authorities had been aroused, and special instructions had been sent that the bags were to be delivered up only to their rightful owners.

It sounds sensible enough. Nobody wants his bag delivered up to anyone else. But it had not been explained to the authorities at Innsbruck how they were to know the proper owners. Three wretched-looking creatures crawled into the post-office and said they wanted those three bags—"those bags, there in the corner"—which happened to be nice, clean, respectable-looking bags, the sort of bags that anyone might want. One of them produced a bit of paper, it is true, which he said had been given to him as a receipt by the post-office people at Constance. But in the lonely passes of the Tyrol one man, set upon by three, might easily be robbed of his papers, and his body thrown over a precipice. The chief clerk shook his head. He would like us to return accompanied by someone who could identify us. The hotel porter occurred to us, as a matter of course. Keeping to the back streets, we returned to the hotel and fished him out of his box.

"I am Mr. J.," I said: "this is my friend Mr. B. and this is Mr. S."

The porter bowed and said he was delighted.

"I want you to come with us to the post-office," I explained, "and identify us."

The hotel porter is always a practical man: his calling robs him of all sympathy with the hide-bound formality of his compatriots. He put on his cap and accompanied us back to the office. He did his best: no one could say he did not. He told them who we were: they asked him how he knew. For reply he asked them how they thought he knew his mother: he just knew us: it was second nature with him. He implied that the question was a silly one, and suggested that, as his time was valuable, they should hand us over the three bags and have done with their nonsense.

They asked him how long he had known us. He threw up his hands with an eloquent gesture: memory refused to travel back such distance. It appeared there was never a time when he had not known us. We had been boys together.

Did he know anybody else who knew us? The question appeared to him almost insulting. Everybody in Innsbruck knew us, honoured us, respected us—everybody, that is, except a few post-office officials, people quite out of society.

Would he kindly bring along, say; one undoubtedly respectable citizen who could vouch for our identity? The request caused him to forget us and our troubles. The argument became a personal quarrel between the porter and the clerk. If he, the porter, was not a respectable citizen of Innsbruck, where was such an one to be found?

[The disadvantage of being an unknown Person.]

Both gentlemen became excited, and the discussion passed beyond my understanding. But I gathered dimly from what the clerk said, that ill-natured remarks relative to the porter's grandfather and a missing cow had never yet been satisfactorily replied to: and, from observations made by the porter, that stories were in circulation about the clerk's aunt and a sergeant of artillery that should suggest to a discreet nephew of the lady the inadvisability of talking about other people's grandfathers.

Our sympathies were naturally with the porter: he was our man, but he did not seem to be advancing our cause much. We left them quarrelling, and persuaded the head waiter that evening to turn out the gas at our end of the table d'hote.

The next morning we returned to the post-office by ourselves. The clerk proved a reasonable man when treated in a friendly spirit. He was a bit of a climber himself. He admitted the possibility of our being the rightful owners. His instructions were only not to DELIVER UP the bags, and he himself suggested a way out of the difficulty. We might come each day and dress in the post-office, behind the screen. It was an awkward arrangement, even although the clerk allowed us the use of the back door. And occasionally, in spite of the utmost care, bits of us would show outside the screen. But for a couple of days, until the British Consul returned from Salzburg, the post-office had to be our dressing room. The continental official, I am inclined to think, errs on the side of prudence.

Jerome K. Jerome

# CHAPTER V

[If only we had not lost our Tails!]

A friend of mine thinks it a pity that we have lost our tails. He argues it would be so helpful if, like the dog, we possessed a tail that wagged when we were pleased, that stuck out straight when we were feeling mad.

"Now, do come and see us again soon," says our hostess; "don't wait to be asked. Drop in whenever you are passing."

We take her at her word. The servant who answers our knocking says she "will see." There is a scuffling of feet, a murmur of hushed voices, a swift opening and closing of doors. We are shown into the drawing-room, the maid, breathless from her search, one supposes, having discovered that her mistress IS at home. We stand upon the hearthrug, clinging to our hat and stick as to things friendly and sympathetic: the suggestion forcing itself upon us is that of a visit to the dentist.

Our hostess enters wreathed in smiles. Is she really pleased to see us, or is she saying to herself, "Drat the man! Why must he choose the very morning I had intended to fix up the clean curtains?"

But she has to pretend to be delighted, and ask us to stay to lunch. It would save us hours of anxiety could we look beyond her smiling face to her tail peeping out saucily from a placket-hole. Is it wagging, or is it standing out rigid at right angles from her skirt?

But I fear by this time we should have taught our tails polite behaviour. We should have schooled them to wag enthusiastically the while we were growling savagely to ourselves. Man put on insincerity to hide his mind when he made himself a garment of fig-leaves to hide his body.

One sometimes wonders whether he has gained so very much. A small acquaintance of mine is being brought up on strange principles. Whether his parents are mad or not is a matter of opinion. Their ideas are certainly peculiar. They encourage him rather than otherwise to tell the truth on all occasions. I am watching the experiment with interest. If you ask him what he thinks of you, he tells you. Some people don't ask him a second time. They say:

"What a very rude little boy you are!"

"But you insisted upon it," he explains; "I told you I'd rather not say."

It does not comfort them in the least. Yet the result is, he is already an influence. People who have braved the ordeal, and emerged successfully, go about with swelled head.

[And little Boys would always tell the Truth!]

Politeness would seem to have been invented for the comfort of the undeserving. We let fall our rain of compliments upon the unjust and the just without distinction. Every hostess has provided us with the most charming evening of our life. Every guest has conferred a like blessing upon us by accepting our invitation. I remember a dear good lady in a small south German town organizing for one winter's day a sleighing party to the woods. A sleighing party differs from a picnic. The people who want each other cannot go off together and lose themselves, leaving the bores to find only each other. You are in close company from early morn till late at night. We were to drive twenty miles, six in a sledge, dine together in a lonely Wirtschaft, dance and sing songs, and afterwards drive home by moonlight. Success depends on every member of the company fitting into his place and assisting in the general harmony. Our chieftainess was fixing the final arrangements the evening before in the drawing-room of the pension. One place was still to spare.

"Tompkins!"

Two voices uttered the name simultaneously; three others immediately took up the refrain. Tompkins was our man—the cheeriest, merriest companion imaginable. Tompkins alone could be trusted to make the affair a success. Tompkins, who had only arrived that afternoon, was pointed out to our chieftainess. We could hear his good-tempered laugh from where we sat, grouped together at the other end of the room. Our chieftainess rose, and made for him direct.

Alas! she was a short-sighted lady—we had not thought of that. She returned in triumph, followed by a dismal-looking man I had met the year before in the Black Forest, and had hoped never to meet again. I drew her aside.

"Whatever you do," I said, "don't ask— " (I forget his name. One of these days I'll forget him altogether, and be happier. I will call him Johnson.) "He would turn the whole thing into a funeral before we were half-way there. I climbed a mountain with him once. He makes you forget all your other troubles; that is the only thing he is good for."

"But who is Johnson?" she demanded. "Why, that's Johnson," I explained—"the thing you've brought over. Why on earth didn't you leave it alone? Where's your woman's instinct?"

"Great heavens!" she cried, "I thought it was Tompkins. I've invited him, and he's accepted."

She was a stickler for politeness, and would not hear of his being told that he had been mistaken for an agreeable man, but that the error, most fortunately, had been discovered in time. He started a row with the driver of the sledge, and devoted the journey outwards to an argument on the fiscal question. He told the proprietor of the hotel what he thought of German cooking, and insisted on having the windows open. One of our party—a German student—sang, "Deutschland, Deutschland uber alles,"—which led to a heated discussion on the proper place of sentiment in literature, and a general denunciation by Johnson of Teutonic characteristics in general. We did not dance. Johnson said that, of course, he spoke only for himself, but the sight of middle-aged ladies and gentlemen catching hold of each other round the middle and jigging about like children was to him rather a saddening spectacle, but to the young such gambolling was natural. Let the young ones indulge themselves. Only four of our party could claim to be under thirty with any hope of success. They were kind enough not to impress the fact upon us. Johnson enlivened the journey back by a searching analysis of enjoyment: Of what did it really consist?

Yet, on wishing him "Good-night," our chieftainess thanked him for his company in precisely the same terms she would have applied to Tompkins, who, by unflagging good humour and tact, would have made the day worth remembering to us all for all time.

[And everyone obtained his just Deserts!]

We pay dearly for our want of sincerity. We are denied the payment of praise: it has ceased to have any value. People shake me warmly by the hand and tell me that they like my books. It only bores me. Not that I am superior to compliment—nobody is—but because I cannot be sure that they mean it. They would say just the same had they never read a line I had written. If I visit a house and find a book of mine open face downwards on the window-seat, it sends no thrill of pride through my suspicious mind. As likely as not, I tell myself, the following is the conversation that has taken place between my host and hostess the day before my arrival:

"Don't forget that man J— is coming down tomorrow."

"To-morrow! I wish you would tell me of these things a little earlier."

"I did tell you—told you last week. Your memory gets worse every day."

"You certainly never told me, or I should have remembered it. Is he anybody important?"

"Oh, no; writes books."

"What sort of books?—I mean, is he quite respectable?"

"Of course, or I should not have invited him. These sort of people go everywhere nowadays. By the by, have we got any of his books about the house?"

"I don't think so. I'll look and see. If you had let me know in time I could have ordered one from Mudie's."

"Well, I've got to go to town; I'll make sure of it, and buy one."

"Seems a pity to waste money. Won't you be going anywhere near Mudie's?"

"Looks more appreciative to have bought a copy. It will do for a birthday present for someone."

On the other hand, the conversation may have been very different. My hostess may have said:

"Oh, I AM glad he's coming. I have been longing to meet him for years."

She may have bought my book on the day of publication, and be reading it through for the second time. She may, by pure accident, have left it on her favourite seat beneath the window. The knowledge that insincerity is our universal garment has reduced all compliment to meaningless formula. A lady one evening at a party drew me aside. The chief guest—a famous writer—had just arrived.

"Tell me," she said, "I have so little time for reading, what has he done?"

I was on the point of replying when an inveterate wag, who had overheard her, interposed between us.

"The Cloister and the Hearth," he told her, "and 'Adam Bede.'"

He happened to know the lady well. She has a good heart, but was ever muddle-headed. She thanked that wag with a smile, and I heard her later in the evening boring most evidently that literary lion with elongated praise of the "Cloister and the Hearth" and "Adam Bede." They were among the few books she had ever read, and talking about them came easily to her. She told me afterwards that she had found that literary lion a charming man, but -

"Well," she laughed, "he has got a good opinion of himself. He told me he considered both books among the finest in the English language."

It is as well always to make a note of the author's name. Some people never do—more particularly playgoers. A well-known dramatic author told me he once took a couple of colonial friends to a play of his own. It was after a little dinner at Kettner's; they suggested the theatre, and he thought he would give them a treat. He did not mention to them that he was the author, and they never looked at the programme. Their faces as the play proceeded lengthened; it did not seem to be their school of comedy. At the end of the first act they sprang to their feet.

"Let's chuck this rot," suggested one.

"Let's go to the Empire," suggested the other. The well-known dramatist followed them out. He thinks the fault must have been with the dinner.

A young friend of mine—a man of good family—contracted a mesalliance: that is, he married the daughter of a Canadian farmer, a frank, amiable girl, bewitchingly pretty, with more character in her little finger than some girls possess in their whole body. I met him one day, some three months after his return to London.

[And only people would do Parlour Tricks who do them well!]

"Well," I asked him, "how is it shaping?"

"She is the dearest girl in the world," he answered. "She has only got one fault; she believes what people say."

"She will get over that," I suggested.

"I hope she does," he replied; "it's awkward at present."

"I can see it leading her into difficulty," I agreed.

"She is not accomplished," he continued. He seemed to wish to talk about it to a sympathetic listener. "She never pretended to be accomplished. I did not marry her for her accomplishments. But now she is beginning to think she must have been accomplished all the time, without knowing it. She plays the piano like a schoolgirl on a parents' visiting-day. She told them she did not play—not worth listening to—at least, she began by telling them so. They insisted that she did, that they had heard about her playing, and were thirsting to enjoy it. She is good nature itself. She would stand on her head if she thought it would give real joy to anyone. She took it they really wanted to hear her, and so let 'em have it. They tell her that her touch is something quite out of the common—which is the truth, if only she could understand it—why did she never think of taking up music as a profession? By this time she is wondering herself that she never did. They are not satisfied with hearing her once. They ask for more, and they get it. The other evening I had to keep quiet on my chair while she thumped through four pieces one after the other, including the Beethoven Sonata. We knew it was the Beethoven Sonata. She told us before she started it was going to be the Beethoven Sonata, otherwise, for all any of us could have guessed, it might have been the 'Battle of Prague.' We all sat round with wooden faces, staring at our boots. Afterwards those of them that couldn't get near enough to her to make a fool of her crowded round me. Wanted to know why I had never told them I had discovered a musical prodigy. I'll lose my temper one day and pull somebody's nose, I feel I shall. She's got a recitation; whether intended to be serious or comic I had never been able to make up my mind. The way she gives it confers upon it all the disadvantages of both. It is chiefly concerned with an angel and a child. But a dog comes into it about the middle, and from that point onward it is impossible to tell who is talking—sometimes you think it is the angel, and then it sounds more like the dog. The child is the easiest to follow: it talks all the time through its nose. If I have heard that recitation once I have heard it fifty times; and now she is busy learning an encore.

[And all the World had Sense!]

"What hurts me most," he went on, "is having to watch her making herself ridiculous. Yet what am I to do? If I explain things to her she will be miserable and ashamed of herself; added to which her frankness—perhaps her greatest charm—will be murdered. The trouble runs through everything. She won't take my advice about her frocks. She laughs, and repeats to me—well, the lies that other women tell a girl who is spoiling herself by dressing absurdly; especially when she is a pretty girl and they are anxious she should go on spoiling

Jerome K. Jerome

herself. She bought a hat last week, one day when I was not with her. It only wants the candles to look like a Christmas tree. They insist on her taking it off so they may examine it more closely, with the idea of having one built like it for themselves; and she sits by delighted, and explains to them the secret of the thing. We get to parties half an hour before the opening time; she is afraid of being a minute late. They have told her that the party can't begin without her—isn't worth calling a party till she's there. We are always the last to go. The other people don't matter, but if she goes they will feel the whole thing has been a failure. She is dead for want of sleep, and they are sick and tired of us; but if I look at my watch they talk as if their hearts were breaking, and she thinks me a brute for wanting to leave friends so passionately attached to us.

"Why do we all play this silly game; what is the sense of it?" he wanted to know.

I could not tell him.

# CHAPTER VI

[Fire and the Foreigner.]

They are odd folk, these foreigners. There are moments of despair when I almost give them up—feel I don't care what becomes of them— feel as if I could let them muddle on in their own way—wash my hands of them, so to speak, and attend exclusively to my own business: we all have our days of feebleness. They will sit outside a cafe on a freezing night, with an east wind blowing, and play dominoes. They will stand outside a tramcar, rushing through the icy air at fifteen miles an hour, and refuse to go inside, even to oblige a lady. Yet in railway carriages, in which you could grill a bloater by the simple process of laying it underneath the seat, they will insist on the window being closed, light cigars to keep their noses warm, and sit with the collars of their fur coats buttoned up around their necks.

In their houses they keep the double windows hermetically sealed for three or four months at a time: and the hot air quivering about the stoves scorches your face if you venture nearer to it than a yard. Travel can broaden the mind. It can also suggest to the Britisher that in some respects his countrymen are nothing near so silly as they are supposed to be. There was a time when I used to sit with my legs stretched out before the English coal fire and listen with respectful attention while people who I thought knew all about it explained to me how wicked and how wasteful were our methods.

Jerome K. Jerome

All the heat from that fire, they told me, was going up the chimney. I did not like to answer them that notwithstanding I felt warm and cosy. I feared it might be merely British stupidity that kept me warm and cosy, not the fire at all. How could it be the fire? The heat from the fire was going up the chimney. It was the glow of ignorance that was making my toes tingle. Besides, if by sitting close in front of the fire and looking hard at it, I did contrive, by hypnotic suggestion, maybe, to fancy myself warm, what should I feel like at the other end of the room?

It seemed like begging the question to reply that I had no particular use for the other end of the room, that generally speaking there was room enough about the fire for all the people I really cared for, that sitting altogether round the fire seemed quite as sensible as sulking by one's self in a corner the other end of the room, that the fire made a cheerful and convenient focus for family and friends. They pointed out to me how a stove, blocking up the centre of the room, with a dingy looking fluepipe wandering round the ceiling, would enable us to sit ranged round the walls, like patients in a hospital waiting-room, and use up coke and potato-peelings.

Since then I have had practical experience of the scientific stove. I want the old-fashioned, unsanitary, wasteful, illogical, open fireplace. I want the heat to go up the chimney, instead of stopping in the room and giving me a headache, and making everything go round. When I come in out of the snow I want to see a fire—something that says to me with a cheerful crackle, "Hallo, old man, cold outside, isn't it? Come and sit down. Come quite close and warm your hands. That's right, put your foot under him and persuade him to move a yard or two. That's all he's been doing for the last hour, lying there roasting himself, lazy little devil. He'll get softening of the spine, that's what will happen to him. Put your toes on the fender. The tea will be here in a minute."

[My British Stupidity.]

I want something that I can toast my back against, while standing with coat tails tucked up and my hands in my pockets, explaining things to people. I don't want a comfortless, staring, white thing, in a corner of the room, behind the sofa—a thing that looks and smells like a family tomb. It may be hygienic, and it may be hot, but it does not seem to do me any good. It has its advantages: it contains a cupboard into which you can put things to dry. You can also forget them, and leave them there. Then people complain of a smell of burning, and hope the house is not on fire, and you ease their mind by explaining to them that it is probably only your boots. Complicated internal arrangements are worked by a key. If you put on too much fuel, and do not work this key properly, the thing explodes. And if you do not put on any coal at all and the fire goes out suddenly, then likewise it explodes. That is the only way it knows of calling attention to itself. On the Continent you know when the fire wants seeing to merely by listening:

"Sounded like the dining-room, that last explosion," somebody remarks.

"I think not," observes another, "I distinctly felt the shock behind me—my bedroom, I expect."

Bits of ceiling begin to fall, and you notice that the mirror over the sideboard is slowly coming towards you.

"Why it must be this stove," you say; "curious how difficult it is to locate sound."

You snatch up the children and hurry out of the room. After a while, when things have settled down, you venture to look in again. Maybe it was only a mild explosion. A ten-pound note and a couple of plumbers in the house for a week will put things right again. They tell me they are economical, these German stoves, but you have got to understand them. I think I have learnt the trick of them at last: and I don't suppose, all told, it has cost me more than fifty pounds. And now I am trying to teach the rest of the family. What I complain about the family is that they do not seem anxious to learn.

"You do it," they say, pressing the coal scoop into my hand: "it makes us nervous."

It is a pretty, patriarchal idea: I stand between the trusting, admiring family and these explosive stoves that are the terror of their lives. They gather round me in a group and watch me, the capable, all-knowing Head who fears no foreign stove. But there are days when I get tired of going round making up fires.

Nor is it sufficient to understand only one particular stove. The practical foreigner prides himself upon having various stoves, adapted to various work. Hitherto I have been speaking only of the stove supposed to be best suited to reception rooms and bedrooms. The hall is provided with another sort of stove altogether: an iron stove this, that turns up its nose at coke and potato-peelings. If you give it anything else but the best coal it explodes. It is like living surrounded by peppery old colonels, trying to pass a peaceful winter among these passionate stoves. There is a stove in the kitchen to be used only for roasting: this one will not look at anything else but wood. Give it a bit of coal, meaning to be kind, and before you are out of the room it has exploded.

Then there is a trick stove specially popular in Belgium. It has a little door at the top and another little door at the bottom, and looks like a pepper-caster. Whether it is happy or not depends upon those two little doors. There are times when it feels it wants the bottom door shut and the top door open, or vice versa, or both open at the same time, or both shut—it is a fussy little stove.

Ordinary intelligence does not help you much with this stove. You want to be bred in the country. It is a question of instinct: you have to have Belgian blood in your veins to get on comfortably with it. On the whole, it is a mild little stove, this Belgian pet. It does not often explode: it only gets angry, and throws its cover into the air, and flings hot coals about the room. It lives, generally speaking, inside an iron cupboard with two doors. When you want it, you open these doors, and pull it out into the room. It works on a swivel. And when you don't want it you try to push it back again, and then the whole thing tumbles over, and the girl throws her hands up to Heaven and says, "Mon Dieu!" and screams for the cook and the femme journee, and they all three say "Mon Dieu!" and fall upon it with buckets of water. By the time everything has been extinguished you have made up your mind to substitute for it just the ordinary explosive stove to which you are accustomed.

[I am considered Cold and Mad.]

In your own house you can, of course, open the windows, and thus defeat the foreign stove. The rest of the street thinks you mad, but then the Englishman is considered by all foreigners to be always mad. It is his privilege to be mad. The street thinks no worse of you than it did before, and you can breathe in comfort. But in the railway carriage they don't allow you to be mad. In Europe, unless you are prepared to draw at sight upon the other passengers, throw the conductor out of the window, and take the train in by yourself, it is useless arguing the question of fresh air. The rule abroad is that if any one man objects to the window being open, the window remains closed. He does not quarrel with you: he rings the bell, and points out to the conductor that the temperature of the carriage has sunk to little more than ninety degrees, Fahrenheit. He thinks a window must be open.

The conductor is generally an old soldier: he understands being shot, he understands being thrown out of window, but not the laws of sanitation. If, as I have explained, you shoot him, or throw him out on the permanent way, that convinces him. He leaves you to discuss the matter with the second conductor, who, by your action, has now, of course, become the first conductor. As there are generally half a dozen of these conductors scattered about the train, the process of educating them becomes monotonous. You generally end by submitting

Jerome K. Jerome

to the law.

Unless you happen to be an American woman. Never did my heart go out more gladly to America as a nation than one spring day travelling from Berne to Vevey. We had been sitting for an hour in an atmosphere that would have rendered a Dante disinclined to notice things. Dante, after ten minutes in that atmosphere, would have lost all interest in the show. He would not have asked questions. He would have whispered to Virgil:

"Get me out of this, old man, there's a good fellow!"

[Sometimes I wish I were an American Woman.]

The carriage was crowded, chiefly with Germans. Every window was closed, every ventilator shut. The hot air quivered round our feet  Seventeen men and four women were smoking, two children were sucking peppermints, and an old married couple were eating their lunch, consisting chiefly of garlic. At a junction, the door was thrown open. The foreigner opens the door a little way, glides in, and closes it behind him. This was not a foreigner, but an American lady, en voyage, accompanied by five other American ladies. They marched in carrying packages. They could not find six seats together, so they scattered up and down the carriage. The first thing that each woman did, the moment she could get her hands free, was to dash for the nearest window and haul it down.

"Astonishes me," said the first woman, "that somebody is not dead in this carriage."

Their idea, I think, was that through asphyxiation we had become comatose, and, but for their entrance, would have died unconscious.

"It is a current of air that is wanted," said another of the ladies.

So they opened the door at the front of the carriage and four of them stood outside on the platform, chatting pleasantly and admiring the scenery, while two of them opened the door at the other end, and took photographs of the Lake of Geneva. The carriage rose and cursed them in six languages. Bells were rung: conductors came flying in. It was all of no use. Those American ladies were cheerful but firm. They argued with volubility: they argued standing in the open doorway. The conductors, familiar, no doubt, with the American lady and her ways, shrugged their shoulders and retired. The other passengers undid their bags and bundles, and wrapped themselves up in shawls and Jaeger nightshirts.

I met the ladies afterwards in Lausanne. They told me they had been condemned to a fine of forty francs apiece. They also explained to me that they had not the slightest intention of paying it.

Jerome K. Jerome

# CHAPTER VII

[Too much Postcard.]

The postcard craze is dying out in Germany—the land of its birth—I am told. In Germany they do things thoroughly, or not at all. The German when he took to sending postcards abandoned almost every other pursuit in life. The German tourist never knew where he had been until on reaching home again he asked some friend or relation to allow him to look over the postcards he had sent. Then it was he began to enjoy his trip.

"What a charming old town!" the German tourist would exclaim. "I wish I could have found time while I was there to have gone outside the hotel and have had a look round. Still, it is pleasant to think one has been there."

"I suppose you did not have much time?" his friend would suggest.

"We did not get there till the evening," the tourist would explain. "We were busy till dark buying postcards, and then in the morning there was the writing and addressing to be done, and when that was over, and we had had our breakfast, it was time to leave again."

He would take up another card showing the panorama from a mountain top.

"Sublime! colossal!" he would cry enraptured. "If I had known it was anything like that, I'd have stopped another day and had a look at it."

It was always worth seeing, the arrival of a party of German tourists in a Schwartzwald village. Leaping from the coach they would surge round the solitary gendarme.

"Where is the postcard shop?" "Tell us—we have only two hours—where do we get postcards?"

The gendarme, scenting Trinkgeld, would head them at the double-quick: stout old gentlemen unaccustomed to the double-quick, stouter Frauen gathering up their skirts with utter disregard to all propriety, slim Fraulein clinging to their beloved would run after him. Nervous pedestrians would fly for safety into doorways, careless loiterers would be swept into the gutter.

In the narrow doorway of the postcard shop trouble would begin. The cries of suffocated women and trampled children, the curses of strong men, would rend the air. The German is a peaceful, law-abiding citizen, but in the hunt for postcards he was a beast. A woman would pounce on a tray of cards, commence selecting, suddenly the tray would be snatched from her. She would burst into tears, and hit the person nearest to her with her umbrella. The cunning and the strong would secure the best cards. The weak and courteous be left with pictures of post offices and railway stations. Torn and dishevelled, the crowd would rush back to the hotel, sweep crockery from the table, and—sucking stumpy pencils—write feverishly. A hurried meal would follow. Then the horses would be put to again, the German tourists would climb back to their places and be driven away, asking of the coachman what the name of the place they had just left might happen to be.

[The Postcard as a Family Curse.]

One presumes that even to the patient German the thing grew tiresome. In the Fliegende Blatter two young clerks were represented discussing the question of summer holidays.

"Where are you going?" asks A of B.

"Nowhere," answers B.

"Can't you afford it?" asks the sympathetic A.

"Only been able to save up enough for the postcards," answers B, gloomily; "no money left for the trip."

Men and women carried bulky volumes containing the names and addresses of the people to whom they had promised to send cards. Everywhere, through winding forest glade, by silver sea, on mountain pathway, one met with prematurely aged looking tourists muttering as they walked:

"Did I send Aunt Gretchen a postcard from that last village that we stopped at, or did I address two to Cousin Lisa?"

Then, again, maybe, the picture postcard led to disappointment. Uninteresting towns clamoured, as ill-favoured spinsters in a photographic studio, to be made beautiful.

"I want," says the lady, "a photograph my friends will really like. Some of these second-rate photographers make one look quite plain. I don't want you to flatter me, if you understand, I merely want something nice."

The obliging photographer does his best. The nose is carefully toned down, the wart becomes a dimple, her own husband doesn't know her. The postcard artist has ended by imagining everything as it might have been.

"If it were not for the houses," says the postcard artist to himself, "this might have been a picturesque old High street of mediaeval aspect."

So he draws a picture of the High street as it might have been. The lover of quaint architecture travels out of his way to see it, and when he finds it and contrasts it with the picture postcard he gets mad. I bought a postcard myself once representing the market place of a certain French town. It seemed to me, looking at the postcard, that I hadn't really seen France—not yet. I travelled nearly a hundred miles to see that market place. I was careful to arrive on market day and to get there at the right time. I reached the market square and looked at it. Then I asked a gendarme where it was.

He said it was there—that I was in it.

I said, "I don't mean this one, I want the other one, the picturesque one."

He said it was the only market square they had. I took the postcard from my pocket.

"Where are all the girls?" I asked him.

"What girls?" he demanded.

[The Artist's Dream.]

"Why, these girls;" I showed him the postcard, there ought to have been about a hundred of them. There was not a plain one among the lot. Many of them I should have called beautiful. They were selling flowers and fruit, all kinds of fruit—cherries, strawberries, rosy- cheeked apples, luscious grapes—all freshly picked and sparkling with dew. The gendarme said he had never seen any girls—not in this particular square. Referring casually to the blood of saints and martyrs, he said he would like to see a few girls in that town worth looking at. In the square itself sat six motherly old souls round a lamp-post. One of them had a moustache, and was smoking a pipe, but in other respects, I have no doubt, was all a woman should be. Two of them were selling fish. That is they would have sold fish, no doubt, had anyone been there to buy fish. The gaily

Jerome K. Jerome

clad thousands of eager purchasers pictured in the postcard were represented by two workmen in blue blouses talking at a corner, mostly with their fingers; a small boy walking backwards, with the idea apparently of not missing anything behind him, and a yellow dog that sat on the kerb, and had given up all hope—judging from his expression—of anything ever happening again. With the gendarme and myself, these four were the only living creatures in the square. The rest of the market consisted of eggs and a few emaciated fowls hanging from a sort of broom handle.

"And where's the cathedral?" I asked the gendarme. It was a Gothic structure in the postcard of evident antiquity. He said there had once been a cathedral. It was now a brewery; he pointed it out to me. He said he thought some portion of the original south wall had been retained. He thought the manager of the brewery might be willing to show it to me.

"And the fountain?" I demanded, "and all these doves!"

He said there had been talk of a fountain. He believed the design had already been prepared.

I took the next train back. I do not now travel much out of my way to see the original of the picture postcard. Maybe others have had like experience and the picture postcard as a guide to the Continent has lost its value.

The dealer has fallen back upon the eternal feminine. The postcard collector is confined to girls. Through the kindness of correspondents I possess myself some fifty to a hundred girls, or perhaps it would be more correct to say one girl in fifty to a hundred different hats. I have her in big hats, I have her in small hats, I have her in no hat at all. I have her smiling, and I have her looking as if she had lost her last sixpence. I have her overdressed, I have her decidedly underdressed, but she is much the same girl. Very young men cannot have too many of her, but myself I am getting tired of her. I suppose it is the result of growing old.

[Why not the Eternal Male for a change?]

Girls of my acquaintance are also beginning to grumble at her. I often think it hard on girls that the artist so neglects the eternal male. Why should there not be portraits of young men in different hats; young men in big hats, young men in little hats, young men smiling archly, young men looking noble. Girls don't want to decorate their rooms with pictures of other girls, they want rows of young men beaming down upon them.

But possibly I am sinning my mercies. A father hears what young men don't. The girl in real life is feeling it keenly: the impossible standard set for her by the popular artist.

"Real skirts don't hang like that," she grumbles, "it's not in the nature of skirts. You can't have feet that size. It isn't our fault, they are not made. Look at those waists! There would be no room to put anything?"

"Nature, in fashioning woman, has not yet crept up to the artistic ideal. The young man studies the picture on the postcard; on the coloured almanack given away at Christmas by the local grocer; on the advertisement of Jones' soap, and thinks with discontent of Polly Perkins, who in a natural way is as pretty a girl as can be looked for in this imperfect world. Thus it is that woman has had to take to shorthand and typewriting. Modern woman is being ruined by the artist.

[How Women are ruined by Art.]

Mr. Anstey tells a story of a young barber who fell in love with his own wax model. All day he dreamed of the impossible. She —the young lady of wax-like complexion, with her everlasting expression of dignity combined with amiability. No girl of his acquaintance could compete with her. If I remember rightly he died a bachelor, still dreaming of wax-like perfection. Perhaps it is as well we men are not handicapped to the same extent. If every hoarding, if every picture shop window, if every illustrated journal teemed with illustrations of the ideal young man in perfect fitting trousers that never bagged at the knees! Maybe it would result in our cooking our own breakfasts and making our own beds to the end of our lives.

The novelist and playwright, as it is, have made things difficult enough for us. In books and plays the young man makes love with a flow of language, a wealth of imagery, that must have taken him years to acquire. What does the novel-reading girl think, I wonder, when the real young man proposes to her! He has not called her anything in particular. Possibly he has got as far as suggesting she is a duck or a daisy, or hinting shyly that she is his bee or his honeysuckle: in his excitement he is not quite sure which. In the novel she has been reading the hero has likened the heroine to half the vegetable kingdom. Elementary astronomy has been exhausted in his attempt to describe to her the impression her appearance leaves on him. Bond Street has been sacked in his endeavour to get it clearly home to her what different parts of her are like—her eyes, her teeth, her heart, her hair, her ears. Delicacy alone prevents his extending the catalogue. A Fiji Island lover might possibly go further. We have not yet had the Fiji Island novel. By the time he is through with it she must have a somewhat confused notion of herself—a vague conviction that she is a sort of condensed South Kensington Museum.

[Difficulty of living up to the Poster.]

Poor Angelina must feel dissatisfied with the Edwin of real life. I am not sure that art and fiction have not made life more difficult for us than even it was intended to be. The view from the mountain top is less extensive than represented by the picture postcard. The play, I fear me, does not always come up to the poster. Polly Perkins is pretty enough as girls go; but oh for the young lady of the grocer's almanack! Poor dear John is very nice and loves us—so he tells us, in his stupid, halting way; but how can we respond when we remember how the man loved in the play! The "artist has fashioned his dream of delight," and the workaday world by comparison seems tame to us.

# CHAPTER VIII

[The Lady and the Problem.]

She is a good woman, the Heroine of the Problem Play, but accidents will happen, and other people were to blame.

Perhaps that is really the Problem: who was responsible for the heroine's past? Was it her father? She does not say so—not in so many words. That is not her way. It is not for her, the silently- suffering victim of complicated antecedent incidents, to purchase justice for herself by pointing the finger of accusation against him who, whatever his faults may be, was once, at all events, her father. That one fact in his favour she can never forget. Indeed she would not if she could. That one asset, for whatever it may be worth by the time the Day of Judgment arrives, he shall retain. It shall not be taken from him. "After all he was my father." She admits it, with the accent on the "was." That he is so no longer, he has only himself to blame. His subsequent behaviour has apparently rendered it necessary for her to sever the relationship.

"I love you," she has probably said to him, paraphrasing Othello's speech to Cassio; "it is my duty, and—as by this time you must be aware—it is my keen if occasionally somewhat involved, sense of duty that is the cause of almost all our troubles in this play. You will always remain the object of what I cannot help feeling is misplaced affection on my part, mingled with contempt. But never more be relative of mine."

Jerome K. Jerome

Certain it is that but for her father she would never have had a past. Failing anyone else on whom to lay the blame for whatever the lady may have done, we can generally fall back upon the father. He becomes our sheet-anchor, so to speak. There are plays in which at first sight it would almost appear there was nobody to blame—nobody, except the heroine herself. It all seems to happen just because she is no better than she ought to be: clearly, the father's fault! for ever having had a daughter no better than she ought to be. As the Heroine of a certain Problem Play once put it neatly and succinctly to the old man himself: "It is you parents that make us children what we are." She had him there. He had not a word to answer for himself, but went off centre, leaving his hat behind him.

Sometimes, however, the father is merely a "Scientist"—which in Stageland is another term for helpless imbecile. In Stageland, if a gentleman has not got to have much brain and you do not know what else to make of him, you let him be a scientist—and then, of course, he is only to blame in a minor degree. If he had not been a scientist—thinking more of his silly old stars or beetles than of his intricate daughter, he might have done something. The heroine does not say precisely what: perhaps have taken her up stairs now and again, while she was still young and susceptible of improvement, and have spanked some sense into her.

[The Stage Hero who, for once, had Justice done to him.]

I remember witnessing long ago, in a country barn, a highly moral play. It was a Problem Play, now I come to think of it. At least, that is, it would have been a Problem Play but that the party with the past happened in this case to be merely a male thing. Stage life presents no problems to the man. The hero of the Problem Play has not got to wonder what to do; he has got to wonder only what the heroine will do next. The hero—he was not exactly the hero; he would have been the hero had he not been hanged in the last act. But for that he was rather a nice young man, full of sentiment and not ashamed of it. From the scaffold he pleaded for leave to embrace his mother just once more before he died. It was a pretty idea. The hangman himself was touched. The necessary leave was granted him. He descended the steps and flung his arms round the sobbing old lady, and—bit off her nose. After that he told her why he had bitten off her nose. It appeared that when he was a boy, he had returned home one evening with a rabbit in his pocket. Instead of putting him across her knee, and working into him the eighth commandment, she had said nothing; but that it seemed to be a fairly useful sort of rabbit, and had sent him out into the garden to pick onions. If she had done her duty by him then, he would not have been now in his present most unsatisfactory position, and she would still have had her nose. The fathers and mothers in the audience applauded, but the children, scenting addition to precedent, looked glum.

Maybe it is something of this kind the heroine is hinting at. Perhaps the Problem has nothing to do with the heroine herself, but with the heroine's parents: what is the best way of bringing up a daughter who shows the slightest sign of developing a tendency towards a Past? Can it be done by kindness? And, if not, how much?

Occasionally the parents attempt to solve the Problem, so far as they are concerned, by dying young—shortly after the heroine's birth. No doubt they argue to themselves this is their only chance of avoiding future blame. But they do not get out of it so easily.

"Ah, if I had only had a mother—or even a father!" cries the heroine: one feels how mean it was of them to slip away as they did.

The fact remains, however, that they are dead. One despises them for dying, but beyond that it is difficult to hold them personally responsible for the heroine's subsequent misdeeds. The argument takes to itself new shape. Is it Fate that is to blame? The lady herself would seem to favour this suggestion. It has always been her fate, she explains, to bring suffering and misery upon those she loves. At first, according to her own account, she rebelled against this cruel Fate—possibly instigated thereto by the people unfortunate enough to he loved by her. But of late she has come to accept this strange destiny of hers with touching resignation. It grieves her, when she thinks of it, that she is unable to imbue those she loves with her own patient spirit. They seem to be a fretful little band.

Considered as a scapegoat, Fate, as compared with the father, has this advantage: it is always about: it cannot slip away and die before the real trouble begins: it cannot even plead a scientific head; it is there all the time. With care one can blame it for most everything. The vexing thing about it is, that it does not mind being blamed. One cannot make Fate feel small and mean. It affords no relief to our harrowed feelings to cry out indignantly to Fate: "look here, what you have done. Look at this sweet and well-proportioned lady, compelled to travel first-class, accompanied by an amount of luggage that must be a perpetual nightmare to her maid, from one fashionable European resort to another; forced to exist on a well-secured income of, apparently, five thousand a year, most of which has to go in clothes; beloved by only the best people in the play; talked about by everybody incessantly to the exclusion of everybody else—all the neighbours interested in her and in nobody else much; all the women envying her; all the men tumbling over one another after her—looks, in spite of all her worries, not a day older than twenty-three; and has discovered a dressmaker never yet known to have been an hour behind her promise! And all your fault, yours, Fate. Will nothing move you to shame?"

[She has a way of mislaying her Husband.]

It brings no satisfaction with it, speaking out one's mind to Fate. We want to see him before us, the thing of flesh and blood that has brought all this upon her. Was it that early husband—or rather the gentleman she thought was her husband. As a matter of fact, he was a husband. Only he did not happen to be hers. That naturally confused her. "Then who is my husband?" she seems to have said to herself; "I had a husband: I remember it distinctly."

"Difficult to know them apart from one another," says the lady with the past, "the way they dress them all alike nowadays. I suppose it does not really matter. They are much the same as one another when you get them home. Doesn't do to be too fussy."

She is a careless woman. She is always mislaying that early husband. And she has an unfortunate knack of finding him at the wrong moment. Perhaps that is the Problem: What is a lady to do with a husband for whom she has no further use? If she gives him away he is sure to come back, like the clever dog that is sent in a hamper to the other end of the kingdom, and three days afterwards is found gasping on the doorstep. If she leaves him in the middle of South Africa, with most of the heavy baggage and all the debts, she may reckon it a certainty that on her return from her next honeymoon he will be the first to greet her.

Her surprise at meeting him again is a little unreasonable. She seems to be under the impression that because she has for-gotten him, he is for all practical purposes dead.

"Why I forgot all about him," she seems to be arguing to herself, "seven years ago at least. According to the laws of Nature there ought to be nothing left of him but just his bones."

She is indignant at finding he is still alive, and lets him know it—tells him he is a beast for turning up at his sister's party, and pleads to him for one last favour: that he will go away where neither she nor anybody else of any importance will ever see him or hear of him again. That's all she asks of him. If he make a point of it she will—though her costume is ill adapted to the exercise—go down upon her knees to ask it of him.

He brutally retorts that he doesn't know where to "get." The lady travels round a good deal and seems to be in most places. She accepts week-end invitations to the houses of his nearest relatives. She has married his first cousin, and is now getting up a bazaar with the help of his present wife. How he is to avoid her he does not quite see.

Perhaps, by the by, that is really the Problem: where is the early husband to disappear to? Even if every time he saw her coming he were to duck under the table, somebody would be sure to notice it and make remarks. Ought he to take himself out one dark night, tie a brick round his neck, and throw himself into a pond?

[What is a Lady to do with a Husband when she has finished with him?]

But men are so selfish. The idea does not even occur to him; and the lady herself is too generous to do more than just hint at it.

Maybe it is Society that is to blame. There comes a luminous moment when it is suddenly revealed to the Heroine of the Problem Play that it is Society that is at the bottom of this thing. She has felt all along there was something the matter. Why has she never thought of it before? Here all these years has she been going about blaming her poor old father; her mother for dying too soon; the remarkable circumstances attending her girlhood; that dear old stupid husband she thought was hers; and all the while the really culpable party has been existing unsuspected under her very nose. She clears away the furniture a bit, and tells Society exactly what she thinks of it—she is always good at that, telling people what she thinks of them. Other people's failings do not escape her, not for long. If Society would only step out for a moment, and look at itself with her eyes, something might be done. If Society, now that the thing has been pointed out to it, has still any lingering desire to live, let it look at her. This, that she is, Society has made her! Let Society have a walk round her, and then go home and reflect.

[Could she—herself—have been to blame?]

It lifts a load from us, fixing the blame on Society. There were periods in the play when we hardly knew what to think. The scientific father, the dead mother, the early husband! it was difficult to grasp the fact that they alone were to blame. One felt there was something to be said for even them. Ugly thoughts would cross our mind that perhaps the Heroine herself was not altogether irreproachable—that possibly there would have been less Problem, if, thinking a little less about her clothes, yearning a little less to do nothing all day long and be perfectly happy, she had pulled herself together, told herself that the world was not built exclusively for her, and settled down to the existence of an ordinary decent woman.

Looking at the thing all round, that is perhaps the best solution of the Problem: it is Society that is to blame. We had better keep to that.

# CHAPTER IX

[Civilization and the Unemployed.]

Where Civilization fails is in not providing men and women with sufficient work. In the Stone Age man was, one imagines, kept busy. When he was not looking for his dinner, or eating his dinner, or sleeping off the effects of his dinner, he was hard at work with a club, clearing the neighbourhood of what one doubts not he would have described as aliens. The healthy Palaeolithic man would have had a contempt for Cobden rivalling that of Mr. Chamberlain himself. He did not take the incursion of the foreigner "lying down." One pictures him in the mind's eye: unscientific, perhaps, but active to a degree difficult to conceive in these degenerate days. Now up a tree hurling cocoa-nuts, the next moment on the ground flinging roots and rocks. Both having tolerably hard heads, the argument would of necessity be long and heated. Phrases that have since come to be meaningless had, in those days, a real significance.

When a Palaeolithic politician claimed to have "crushed his critic," he meant that he had succeeded in dropping a tree or a ton of earth upon him. When it was said that one bright and intelligent member of that early sociology had "annihilated his opponent," that opponent's friends and relations took no further interest in him. It meant that he was actually annihilated. Bits of him might be found, but the most of him would be hopelessly scattered. When the adherents of any particular Cave Dweller remarked that their man was wiping the floor with his rival, it did not mean that he was talking himself red in the face to a bored audience of sixteen friends and a reporter. It meant that he was dragging that rival by the legs round the enclosure and making the place damp and untidy with him.

[Early instances of "Dumping."]

Maybe the Cave Dweller, finding nuts in his own neighbourhood growing scarce, would emigrate himself: for even in that age the politician was not always logical. Thus roles became reversed. The defender of his country became the alien, dumping himself where he was not wanted. The charm of those early political arguments lay in their simplicity. A child could have followed every point. There could never have been a moment's doubt, even among his own followers, as to what a Palaeolithic statesman really meant to convey. At the close of the contest the party who considered it had won the moral victory would be cleared away, or buried neatly on the spot, according to taste: and the discussion, until the arrival of the next generation, was voted closed.

All this must have been harassing, but it did serve to pass away the time. Civilization has brought into being a section of the community with little else to do but to amuse itself. For youth to play is natural; the young barbarian plays, the kitten plays, the colt gambols, the lamb skips. But man is the only animal that gambols and jumps and skips after it has reached maturity. Were we to meet an elderly bearded goat, springing about in the air and behaving, generally speaking, like a kid, we should say it had gone mad. Yet we throng in our thousands to watch elderly ladies and gentlemen jumping about after a ball, twisting themselves into strange shapes, rushing, racing, falling over one another; and present them with silver-backed hair-brushes and gold-handled umbrellas as a reward to them for doing so.

Imagine some scientific inhabitant of one of the larger fixed stars examining us through a magnifying-glass as we examine ants. Our amusements would puzzle him. The ball of all sorts and sizes, from the marble to the pushball, would lead to endless scientific argument.

"What is it? Why are these men and women always knocking it about, seizing it wherever and whenever they find it and worrying it?"

The observer from that fixed star would argue that the Ball must be some malignant creature of fiendish power, the great enemy of the human race. Watching our cricket-fields, our tennis-courts, our golf links, he would conclude that a certain section of mankind had been told off to do battle with the "Ball" on behalf of mankind in general.

"As a rule," so he would report, "it is a superior class of insect to which this special duty has been assigned. They are a friskier, gaudier species than their fellows.

[Cricket, as viewed from the fixed Stars.]

"For this one purpose they appear to be kept and fed. They do no other work, so far as I have been able to ascertain. Carefully selected and trained, their mission is to go about the world looking for Balls. Whenever they find a Ball they set to work to kill it. But the vitality of these Balls is extraordinary. There is a medium-sized, reddish species that, on an average, takes three days to kill. When one of these is discovered, specially trained champions are summoned from every corner of the country. They arrive in hot haste, eager for the battle, which takes place in the presence of the entire neighbourhood. The number of champions for some reason or another is limited to twenty-two. Each one seizing in turn a large piece of wood, rushes at the Ball as it flies along the ground, or through the air, and strikes at it with all his force. When, exhausted, he can strike no longer, he throws down his weapon and retires into a tent, where he is restored to strength by copious draughts of a drug the nature of which I have been unable to discover. Meanwhile, another has picked up the fallen weapon, and the contest is continued without a moment's interruption. The Ball makes frantic efforts to escape from its tormentors, but every time it is captured and flung back. So far as can be observed, it makes no attempt at retaliation, its only object being to get away; though, occasionally—whether by design or accident—it succeeds in inflicting injury upon one or other of its executioners, or more often upon one of the spectators, striking him either on the head or about the region of the waist, which, judging by results, would appear, from the Ball's point of view, to be the better selection. These small reddish Balls are quickened into life evidently by the heat of the sun; in the cold season they disappear, and their place is taken by a much larger Ball. This Ball the champions kill by striking it with their feet and with their heads. But sometimes they will attempt to suffocate it by falling on it, some dozen of them at a time.

"Another of these seemingly harmless enemies of the human race is a small white Ball of great cunning and resource. It frequents sandy districts by the sea coast and open spaces near the large towns. It is pursued with extraordinary animosity by a florid-faced insect of fierce aspect and rotundity of figure. The weapon he employs is a long stick loaded with metal. With one blow he will send the creature through the air sometimes to a distance of nearly a quarter of a mile; yet so vigorous is the constitution of these Balls that it will fall to earth apparently but little damaged. It is followed by the rotund man accompanied by a smaller insect carrying spare clubs. Though hampered by the prominent whiteness of its skin, the extreme smallness of this Ball often enables it to defy re-discovery, and at such times the fury of the little round man is terrible to contemplate. He dances round the spot where the ball has disappeared, making frenzied passes at the surrounding vegetation with his club, uttering the while the most savage and bloodcurdling growls. Occasionally striking at the small creature in fury, he will miss it altogether, and, having struck merely the air, will sit down heavily upon the ground, or, striking the solid earth, will shatter his own club. Then a curious thing takes place: all the other insects standing round place their right hand before their mouth, and, turning away their faces, shake their bodies to and fro, emitting a strange crackling sound. Whether this is to be regarded as a mere expression of their grief that the blow of their comrade should have miscarried, or whether one may assume it to be a ceremonious appeal to their gods for better luck next time, I have not as yet made up my mind. The striker, meanwhile, raises both arms, the hands tightly clenched, towards the heavens, and utters what is probably a prayer, prepared expressly for the occasion.

[The Heir of all Ages. His Inheritance.]

In similar manner he, the Celestial Observer, proceeds to describe our billiard matches, our tennis tournaments, our croquet parties. Maybe it never occurs to him that a large section of our race surrounded by Eternity, would devote its entire span of life to sheer killing of time. A middle-aged friend of mine, a cultured gentleman, a M.A. of Cambridge, assured me the other day that, notwithstanding all his experiences of life, the thing that still gave him the greatest satisfaction was the accomplishment of a successful drive to leg. Rather a quaint commentary on our civilization, is it not? "The singers have sung, and the builders have builded. The artists have fashioned their dreams of delight." The martyrs for thought and freedom have died their death; knowledge has sprung from the bones of ignorance; civilization for ten thousand years has battled with brutality to this result—that a specimen gentleman of the Twentieth Century, the heir of all the ages, finds his greatest joy in life the striking of a ball with a chunk of wood!

Human energy, human suffering, has been wasted. Such crown of happiness for a man might surely have been obtained earlier and at less cost. Was it intended? Are we on the right track? The child's play is wiser. The battered doll is a princess. Within the sand castle dwells an ogre. It is with imagination that he plays. His games have some relation to life. It is the man only who is content with this everlasting knocking about of a ball. The majority of mankind is doomed to labour so constant, so exhausting, that no opportunity is given it to cultivate its brain. Civilization has arranged that a small privileged minority shall alone enjoy that leisure necessary to the development of thought. And what is the answer of this leisured class? It is:

"We will do nothing for the world that feeds us, clothes us, keeps us in luxury. We will spend our whole existence knocking balls about, watching other people knocking balls about, arguing with one another as to the best means of knocking balls about."

[Is it "Playing the Game?"]

Is it—to use their own jargon—"playing the game?"

And the queer thing is this over-worked world, that stints itself to keep them in idleness, approves of the answer. "The flannelled fool," "The muddied oaf," is the pet of the people; their hero, their ideal.

But maybe all this is mere jealousy. Myself, I have never been clever at knocking balls about.

Jerome K. Jerome

# CHAPTER X

[Patience and the Waiter.]

The slowest waiter I know is the British railway refreshment-room waiter.

His very breathing—regular, harmonious, penetrating, instinct as it is with all the better attributes of a well-preserved grandfather's clock—conveys suggestion of dignity and peace. He is a huge, impressive person. There emanates from him an atmosphere of Lotusland. The otherwise unattractive refreshment-room becomes an oasis of repose amid the turmoil of a fretful world. All things conspire to aid him: the ancient joints, ranged side by side like corpses in a morgue, each one decently hidden under its white muslin shroud, whispering of death and decay; the dish of dead flies, thoughtfully placed in the centre of the table; the framed advertisements extolling the virtues of heavy beers and stouts, of weird champagnes, emanating from haunted-looking chateaux, situate—if one may judge from the illustration—in the midst of desert lands; the sleep-inviting buzz of the bluebottles.

The spirit of the place steals over you. On entering, with a quarter of an hour to spare, your idea was a cutlet and a glass of claret. In the face of the refreshment-room waiter, the notion appears frivolous, not to say un-English. You order cold beef and pickles, with a pint of bitter in a tankard. To win the British waiter's approval, you must always order beer in a tankard. The British waiter, in his ideals, is mediaeval. There is a Shakespearean touch about a tankard. A soapy potato will, of course, be added. Afterwards a ton of cheese and a basin of rabbit's food floating in water (the British salad) will be placed before you. You will work steadily through the whole, anticipating the somnolence that will subsequently fall upon you with a certain amount of satisfaction. It will serve to dispel the last lingering regret at the reflection that you will miss your appointment, and suffer thereby serious inconvenience if not positive loss. These things are of the world—the noisy, tiresome world you have left without.

To the English traveller, the foreign waiter in the earlier stages of his career is a burden and a trial. When he is complete— when he really can talk English I rejoice in him. When I object to him is when his English is worse than my French or German, and when he will, for his own educational purposes, insist, nevertheless, that the conversation shall be entirely in English. I would he came to me some other time. I would so much rather make it after dinner or, say, the next morning. I hate giving lessons during meal times.

Besides, to a man with feeble digestion, this sort of thing can lead to trouble. One waiter I met at an hotel in Dijon knew very little English—about as much as a poll parrot. The moment I entered the salle-a-manger he started to his feet.

"Ah! You English!" he cried.

"Well, what about us?" I answered. It was during the period of the Boer War. I took it he was about to denounce the English nation generally. I was looking for something to throw at him.

"You English—you Englishman, yes," he repeated.

And then I understood he had merely intended a question. I owned up that I was, and accused him in turn of being a Frenchman. He admitted it. Introductions, as it were, thus over, I thought I would order dinner. I ordered it in French. I am not bragging of my French, I never wanted to learn

French. Even as a boy, it was more the idea of others than of myself. I learnt as little as possible. But I have learnt enough to live in places where they can't, or won't, speak anything else. Left to myself, I could have enjoyed a very satisfactory dinner. I was tired with a long day's journey, and hungry. They cook well at this hotel. I had been looking forward to my dinner for hours and hours. I had sat down in my imagination to a consomme bisque, sole au gratin, a poulet saute, and an omelette au fromage.

[Waiterkind in the making.]

It is wrong to let one's mind dwell upon carnal delights; I see that now. At the time I was mad about it. The fool would not even listen to me. He had got it into his garlic-sodden brain that all Englishmen live on beef, and nothing but beef. He swept aside all my suggestions as though they had been the prattlings of a foolish child.

"You haf nice biftek. Not at all done. Yes?"

"No, I don't," I answered. "I don't want what the cook of a French provincial hotel calls a biftek. I want something to eat. I want—" Apparently, he understood neither English nor French.

"Yes, yes," he interrupted cheerfully, "with pottitoes."

"With what?" I asked. I thought for the moment he was suggesting potted pigs' feet in the nearest English he could get to it.

"Pottito," he repeated; "boil pottito. Yes? And pell hell."

I felt like telling him to go there; I suppose he meant "pale ale." It took me about five minutes to get that beefsteak out of his head. By the time I had done it, I did not care what I had for dinner. I took pot-du-jour and veal. He added, on his own initiative, a thing that looked like a poultice. I did not try the taste of it. He explained it was "plum poodeen." I fancy he had made it himself.

This fellow is typical; you meet him everywhere abroad. He translates your bill into English for you, calls ten centimes a penny, calculates twelve francs to the pound, and presses a handful of sous affectionately upon you as change for a napoleon.

The cheating waiter is common to all countries, though in Italy and Belgium he flourishes, perhaps, more than elsewhere. But the British waiter, when detected, becomes surly—does not take it nicely. The foreign waiter is amiable about it—bears no malice. He is grieved, maybe, at your language, but that is because he is thinking of you—the possible effect of it upon your future. To try and stop you, he offers you another four sous. The story is told of a Frenchman who, not knowing the legal fare, adopted the plan of doling out pennies to a London cabman one at a time, continuing until the man looked satisfied. Myself, I doubt the story. From what I know of the London cabman, I can see him leaning down still, with out-stretched hand, the horse between the shafts long since dead, the cab chockfull of coppers, and yet no expression of satiety upon his face.

But the story would appear to have crossed the Channel, and to have commended itself to the foreign waiter—especially to the railway refreshment-room waiter. He doles out sous to the traveller, one at a time, with the air of a man who is giving away the savings of a lifetime. If, after five minutes or so, you still appear discontented he goes away quite suddenly. You think he has gone to open another chest of half-pence, but when a quarter of an hour has passed and he does not reappear, you inquire about him amongst the other waiters.

A gloom at once falls upon them. You have spoken of the very thing that has been troubling them. He used to be a waiter here once—one might almost say until quite recently. As to what has become of him- -ah! there you have them. If in the course of their chequered career they ever come across him, they will mention to him that you are waiting for him. Meanwhile a stentorian-voiced official is shouting that your train is on the point of leaving. You console yourself with the reflection that it might have been more. It always might have been more; sometimes it is.

[His Little Mistakes.]

A waiter at the Gare du Nord, in Brussels, on one occasion pressed upon me a five-franc piece, a small Turkish coin the value of which was unknown to me, and remains so to this day, a distinctly bad two francs, and from a quarter of a pound to six ounces of centimes, as change for a twenty-franc note, after deducting the price of a cup of coffee. He put it down with the air of one subscribing to a charity. We looked at one another. I suppose I must have conveyed to him the impression of being discontented. He drew a purse from his pocket. The action suggested that, for the purpose of satisfying my inordinate demands, he would be compelled to draw upon his private resources; but it did not move me. Abstracting reluctantly a fifty-centime piece, he added it to the heap upon the table.

I suggested his taking a seat, as at this rate it seemed likely we should be doing business together for some time. I think he gathered I was not a fool. Hitherto he had been judging, I suppose, purely from appearances. But he was not in the least offended.

"Ah!" he cried, with a cheery laugh, "Monsieur comprend!" He swept the whole nonsense back into his bag and gave me the right change. I slipped my arm through his and insisted upon the pleasure of his society, until I had examined each and every coin. He went away chuckling, and told another waiter all about it. They both of them bowed to me as I went out, and wished me a pleasant journey. I left them still chuckling. A British waiter would have been sulky all the afternoon.

The waiter who insists upon mistaking you for the heir of all the Rothschilds used to cost me dear when I was younger. I find the best plan is to take him in hand at the beginning and disillusion him; sweep aside his talk of '84 Perrier Jouet, followed by a '79 Chateau Lafite, and ask him, as man to man, if he can conscientiously recommend the Saint Julien at two-and-six. After that he settles down to his work and talks sense.

The fatherly waiter is sometimes a comfort. You feel that he knows best. Your instinct is to address him as "Uncle." But you remember yourself in time. When you are dining a lady, however, and wish to appear important, he is apt to be in the way. It seems, somehow, to be his dinner. You have a sense almost of being de trop.

The greatest insult you can offer a waiter is to mistake him for your waiter. You think he is your waiter—there is the bald head, the black side-whiskers, the Roman nose. But your waiter had blue eyes, this man soft hazel. You had forgotten to notice the eyes. You bar his progress and ask him for the red pepper. The haughty contempt with which he regards you is painful to bear. It is as if you had insulted a lady. He appears to be saying the same thing:

"I think you have made a mistake. You are possibly confusing me with somebody else; I have not the honour of your acquaintance."

[How to insult him.]

I do not wish it to be understood that I am in the habit of insulting ladies, but occasionally I have made an innocent mistake, and have met with some such response. The wrong waiter conveys to me precisely the same feeling of humiliation.

"I will send your waiter to you," he answers. His tone implies that there are waiters and waiters; some may not mind what class of person they serve: others, though poor, have their self-respect. It is clear to you now why your waiter is keeping away from you; the man is ashamed of being your waiter. He is watching, probably, for an opportunity to approach you when nobody is looking. The other waiter finds him for you. He was hiding behind a screen.

"Table forty-two wants you," the other tells him. The tone of voice adds:

"If you like to encourage this class of customer that is your business; but don't ask me to have anything to do with him."

Even the waiter has his feelings.

# CHAPTER XI

[The everlasting Newness of Woman.]

An Oriental visitor was returning from our shores to his native land.

"Well," asked the youthful diplomatist who had been told off to show him round, as on the deck of the steamer they shook hands, "what do you now think of England?"

"Too much woman," answered the grave Orientalist, and descended to his cabin.

The young diplomatist returned to the shore thoughtful, and later in the day a few of us discussed the matter in a far-off, dimly-lighted corner of the club smoking-room.

Has the pendulum swung too far the other way? Could there be truth in our Oriental friend's terse commentary? The eternal feminine! The Western world has been handed over to her. The stranger from Mars or Jupiter would describe us as a hive of women, the sober-clad male being retained apparently on condition of its doing all the hard work and making itself generally useful. Formerly it was the man who wore the fine clothes who went to the shows. To-day it is the woman gorgeously clad for whom the shows are organized. The man dressed in a serviceable and unostentatious, not to say depressing, suit of black accompanies her for the purpose of carrying her cloak and calling her carriage. Among the working

Jerome K. Jerome

classes life, of necessity, remains primitive; the law of the cave is still, with slight modification, the law of the slum. But in upper and middle-class circles the man is now the woman's servant.

I remember being present while a mother of my acquaintance was instilling into the mind of her little son the advantages of being born a man. A little girl cousin was about to spend a week with him. It was impressed upon him that if she showed a liking for any of his toys, he was at once to give them up to her.

"But why, mamma?" he demanded, evidently surprised.

"Because, my dear, you are a little man."

Should she break them, he was not to smack her head or kick her—as his instinct might prompt him to do. He was just to say:

"Oh, it is of no consequence at all," and to look as if he meant it.

[Doctor says she is not to be bothered.]

She was always to choose the game—to have the biggest apple. There was much more of a similar nature. It was all because he was a little man and she was a little woman. At the end he looked up, puzzled:

"But don't she do anything, 'cos she's a little girl?"

It was explained to him that she didn't. By right of being born a little girl she was exempt from all duty.

Woman nowadays is not taking any duty. She objects to housekeeping; she calls it domestic slavery, and feels she was intended for higher things. What higher things she does not condescend to explain. One or two wives of my acquaintance have persuaded their husbands that these higher things are all-important. The home has been given up. In company with other strivers after higher things, they live now in dismal barracks differing but little from a glorified Bloomsbury lodging-house. But they call them "Mansions" or "Courts," and seem proud of the address. They are not bothered with servants—with housekeeping. The idea of the modern woman is that she is not to be bothered with anything. I remember the words with which one of these ladies announced her departure from her bothering home.

"Oh, well, I'm tired of trouble," she confided to another lady, "so I've made up my mind not to have any more of it."

Artemus Ward tells us of a man who had been in prison for twenty years. Suddenly a bright idea occurred to him; he opened the window and got out. Here have we poor, foolish mortals been imprisoned in this troublesome world for Lord knows how many millions of years. We have got so used to trouble we thought there was no help for it. We have told ourselves that "Man is born to trouble as the sparks fly upwards." We imagined the only thing to be done was to bear it philosophically. Why did not this bright young creature come along before—show us the way out. All we had to do was to give up the bothering home and the bothering servants, and go into a "Mansion" or a "Court."

It seems that you leave trouble outside—in charge of the hall-porter, one supposes. He ties it up for you as the Commissionaire of the Army and Navy Stores ties up your dog. If you want it again, you ask for it as you come out. Small wonder that the "Court" and "Mansion" are growing in popularity every day.

[That "Higher Life."]

They have nothing to do now all day long, these soaring wives of whom I am speaking. They would scorn to sew on a shirt-button even. Are there not other women—of an inferior breed—specially fashioned by Providence for the doing of such slavish tasks? They have no more bothers of any kind. They are free to lead the higher life. What I am waiting for is a glimpse of the higher life. One of them, it is true, has taken up the violin. Another of them is devoting her emancipation to poker work. A third is learning skirt-dancing. Are these the "higher things" for which women are claiming freedom from all duty? And, if so, is there not danger that the closing of our homes may lead to the crowding up of the world with too much higher things?

May there not, by the time all bothers have been removed from woman's path, be too many amateur violinists in the world, too many skirt- dancers, too much poker work? If not, what are they? these "higher things," for which so many women are demanding twenty-four hours a day leisure. I want to know.

One lady of my acquaintance is a Poor Law Guardian and secretary to a labour bureau. But then she runs a house with two servants, four children, and a husband, and appears to be so used to bothers that she would feel herself lost without them. You can do this kind of work apparently even when you are bothered with a home. It is the skirt-dancing and the poker work that cannot brook rivalry. The modern woman has begun to find children a nuisance; they interfere with her development. The mere man, who has written his poems, painted his pictures, composed his melodies, fashioned his philosophies, in the midst of life's troubles and bothers, grows nervous thinking what this new woman must be whose mind is so tremendous that the whole world must be shut up, so to speak, sent to do its business out of her sight and hearing, lest her attention should be distracted.

An optimistic friend of mine tells me not to worry myself; tells me that it is going to come out all right in the end. Woman just now, he contends, is passing through her college period. The school life of strict surveillance is for ever done with. She is now the young Freshwoman. The bothering lessons are over, the bothering schoolmaster she has said good-bye to. She has her latchkey and is "on her own." There are still some bothering rules about being in at twelve o'clock, and so many attendances each term at chapel. She is indignant. This interferes with her idea that life is to be one long orgie of self-indulgence, of pleasure. The college period will pass—is passing. Woman will go out into the world, take her place there, discover that bothers were not left behind in the old schoolhouse, will learn that life has duties, responsibilities, will take up her burden side by side with man, will accomplish her destiny.

[Is there anything left for her to learn?]

Meanwhile, however, she is having a good time—some people think too good a time. She wants the best of both. She demands the joys of independence together with freedom from all work—slavery she calls it. The servants are not to be allowed to bother her, the children are not to be allowed to bother her, her husband is not to be allowed to bother her. She is to be free to lead the higher life. My dear lady, we all want to lead the higher life. I don't want to write these articles. I want somebody else to bother about my rates and taxes, my children's boots, while I sit in an easy-chair and dream about the wonderful books I am going to write, if only a stupid public would let me. Tommy Smith of Brixton feels that he was intended for higher things. He does not want to be wasting his time in an office from nine to six adding up figures. His proper place in life is that of Prime Minister or Field Marshal: he feels it. Do you think the man has no yearning for higher things? Do you think we like the office, the shop, the factory? We ought to be writing poetry, painting pictures, the whole world admiring us. You seem to imagine your man goes off every morning to a sort of City picnic, has eight hours' fun—which he calls work—and then comes home to annoy you with chatter about dinner.

It is the old fable reversed; man said woman had nothing to do all day but to enjoy herself. Making a potato pie! What sort of work was that? Making a potato pie was a lark; anybody could make a potato pie.

So the woman said, "Try it," and took the man's spade and went out into the field, and left him at home to make that pie.

The man discovered that potato pies took a bit more making than he had reckoned—found that running the house and looking after the children was not quite the merry pastime he had argued. Man was a fool.

Now it is the woman who talks without thinking. How did she like hoeing the potato patch? Hard work, was it not, my dear lady? Made your back ache? It came on to rain and you got wet.

I don't see that it very much matters which of you hoes the potato patch, which of you makes the potato pie. Maybe the hoeing of the patch demands more muscle—is more suited to the man. Maybe the making of the pie may be more in your department. But, as I have said, I cannot see that this matter is of importance. The patch has to be hoed, the pie to be cooked; the one cannot do the both. Settle it between you, and, having settled it, agree to do each your own work free from this everlasting nagging.

I know, personally, three ladies who have exchanged the woman's work for the man's. One was deserted by her husband, and left with two young children. She hired a capable woman to look after the house, and joined a ladies' orchestra as pianist at two pounds a week. She now earns four, and works twelve hours a day. The husband of the second fell ill. She set him to write letters and run errands, which was light work that he could do, and started a dressmaker's business. The third was left a widow without means. She sent her three children to boarding-school, and opened a tea-room. I don't know how they talked before, but I know that they do not talk now as though earning the income was a sort of round game.

[When they have tried it the other way round.]

On the Continent they have gone deliberately to work, one would imagine, to reverse matters. Abroad woman is always where man ought to be, and man where most ladies would prefer to meet with women. The ladies garde-robe is superintended by a superannuated sergeant of artillery. When I want to curl my moustache, say, I have to make application to a superb golden-haired creature, who stands by and watches me with an interested smile. I would be much happier waited on by the superannuated sergeant, and my wife tells me she could very well spare him. But it is the law of the land. I remember the first time I travelled with my daughter on the Continent. In the morning I was awakened by a piercing scream from her room. I struggled into my pyjamas, and rushed to her assistance. I could not see her. I could see nothing but a muscular-looking man in a blue blouse with a can of hot water in one hand and a pair of boots in the other. He appeared to be equally bewildered with myself at the sight of the empty bed. From a cupboard in the corner came a wail of distress:

"Oh, do send that horrid man away. What's he doing in my room?"

I explained to her afterwards that the chambermaid abroad is always an active and willing young man. The foreign girl fills in her time bricklaying and grooming down the horses. It is a young and charming lady who serves you when you enter the tobacconist's. She doesn't understand tobacco, is unsympathetic; with Mr. Frederic Harrison, regards smoking as a degrading and unclean habit; cannot see, herself, any difference between shag and Mayblossom, seeing that they are both the same price; thinks you fussy. The corset shop is run by a most presentable young man in a Vandyck beard. The wife runs the restaurant; the man does the cooking, and yet the woman has not reached freedom from bother.

[A brutal suggestion]

Jerome K. Jerome

It sounds brutal, but perhaps woman was not intended to live free from all bothers. Perhaps even the higher life—the skirt-dancing and the poker work—has its bothers. Perhaps woman was intended to take her share of the world's work—of the world's bothers.

# CHAPTER XII

[Why I hate Heroes]

When I was younger, reading the popular novel used to make me sad. I find it vexes others also. I was talking to a bright young girl upon the subject not so very long ago.

"I just hate the girl in the novel," she confessed. "She makes me feel real bad. If I don't think of her I feel pleased with myself, and good; but when I read about her—well, I'm crazy. I would not mind her being smart, sometimes. We can all of us say the right thing, now and then. This girl says them straight away, all the time. She don't have to dig for them even; they come crowding out of her. There never happens a time when she stands there feeling like a fool and knowing that she looks it. As for her hair: 'pon my word, there are days when I believe it is a wig. I'd like to get behind her and give it just one pull. It curls of its own accord. She don't seem to have any trouble with it. Look at this mop of mine. I've been working at it for three-quarters of an hour this morning; and now I would not laugh, not if you were to tell me the funniest thing, you'd ever heard, for fear it would come down again. As for her clothes, they make me tired. She don't possess a frock that does not fit her to perfection; she doesn't have to think about them. You would imagine she went into the garden and picked them off a tree. She just slips it on and comes down, and then—my stars! All the other women in the room may just as well go to bed and get a good night's rest for all the chance they've got. It isn't that she's beautiful. From what they tell

Jerome K. Jerome

you about her, you might fancy her a freak. Looks don't appear to matter to her; she gets there anyhow. I tell you she just makes me boil."

Allowing for the difference between the masculine and feminine outlook, this is precisely how I used to feel when reading of the hero. He was not always good; sometimes he hit the villain harder than he had intended, and then he was sorry—when it was too late, blamed himself severely, and subscribed towards the wreath. Like the rest of us, he made mistakes; occasionally married the wrong girl. But how well he did everything!—does still for the matter of that, I believe. Take it that he condescends to play cricket! He never scores less than a hundred—does not know how to score less than a hundred, wonders how it could be done, supposing, for example, you had an appointment and wanted to catch an early train. I used to play cricket myself, but I could always stop at ten or twenty. There have been times when I have stopped at even less.

It is the same with everything he puts his hand to. Either he does not care for boating at all, or, as a matter of course, he pulls stroke in the University Boat-race; and then takes the train on to Henley and wins the Diamond Sculls so easily that it hardly seems worth while for the other fellow to have started. Were I living in Novel-land, and had I entered for the Diamond Sculls, I should put it to my opponent before the word was given to us to go.

"One minute!" I should have called out to him. "Are you the hero of this novel, or, like myself, only one of the minor characters? Because, if you are the hero you go on; don't you wait for me. I shall just pull as far as the boathouse and get myself a cup of tea."

[Because it always seems to be his Day.]

There is no sense of happy medium about the hero of the popular novel. He cannot get astride a horse without its going off and winning a steeplechase against the favourite. The crowd in Novel- land appears to have no power of observation. It worries itself about the odds, discusses records, reads the nonsense published by the sporting papers. Were I to find myself on a racecourse in Novel- land I should not trouble about the unessential; I should go up to the bookie who looked as if he had the most money, and should say to him:

"Don't shout so loud; you are making yourself hoarse. Just listen to me. Who's the hero of this novel? Oh, that's he, is it? The heavy- looking man on the little brown horse that keeps coughing and is suffering apparently from bone spavin? Well, what are the odds against his winning by ten lengths? A thousand to one! Very well! Have you got a bag?—Good. Here's twenty-seven pounds in gold and eighteen shillings in silver. Coat and waistcoat, say another ten shillings. Shirt and trousers—it's all right, I've got my pyjamas on underneath— say seven and six. Boots—we won't quarrel—make it five bob. That's twenty-nine pounds and sixpence, isn't it? In addition here's a mortgage on the family estate, which I've had made out in blank, an I O U for fourteen pounds which has been owing to me now for some time, and this bundle of securities which, strictly speaking, belong to my Aunt Jane. You keep that little lot till after the race, and we will call it in round figures, five hundred pounds."

That single afternoon would thus bring me in five hundred thousand pounds—provided the bookie did not blow his brains out.

Backers in Novel-land do not seem to me to know their way about. If the hero of the popular novel swims at all, it is not like an ordinary human being that he does it. You never meet him in a swimming-bath; he never pays ninepence, like the rest of us, for a machine. He goes out at uncanny hours, generally accompanied by a lady friend, with whom the while swimming he talks poetry and cracks jokes. Some of us, when we try to talk in the sea, fill ourselves up with salt water. This chap lies on his back and carols, and the wild waves, seeing him, go round the other way. At billiards he can give the average sharper forty in a hundred. He does not really want to play; he does it to teach these bad men a lesson. He has not handled a cue for years. He picked up the game when a young man in Australia, and it seems to have lingered with him.

He does not have to get up early and worry dumb-bells in his nightshirt; he just lies on a sofa in an elegant attitude and muscle comes to him. If his horse declines to jump a hedge, he slips down off the animal's back and throws the poor thing over; it saves argument. If he gets cross and puts his shoulder to the massive oaken door, we know there is going to be work next morning for the carpenter. Maybe he is a party belonging to the Middle Ages. Then when he reluctantly challenges the crack fencer of Europe to a duel, our instinct is to call out and warn his opponent.

"You silly fool," one feels one wants to say; "why, it is the hero of the novel! You take a friend's advice while you are still alive, and get out of it anyway—anyhow. Apologize—hire a horse and cart, do something. You're not going to fight a duel, you're going to commit suicide."

If the hero is a modern young man, and has not got a father, or has only something not worth calling a father, then he comes across a library—anybody's library does for him. He passes Sir Walter Scott and the "Arabian Nights," and makes a bee-line for Plato; it seems to be an instinct with him. By help of a dictionary he worries it out in the original Greek. This gives him a passion for Greek.

When he has romped through the Greek classics he plays about among the Latins. He spends most of his spare time in that library, and forgets to go to tea.

[Because he always "gets there," without any trouble.]

That is the sort of boy he is. How I used to hate him! If he has a proper sort of father, then he goes to college. He does no work: there is no need for him to work: everything seems to come to him. That was another grievance of mine against him. I always had to work a good deal, and very little came of it. He fools around doing things that other men would be sent down for; but in his case the professors love him for it all the more. He is the sort of man who can't do wrong. A fortnight before the examination he ties a wet towel round his head. That is all we hear about it. It seems to be the towel that does it. Maybe, if the towel is not quite up to its work, he will help things on by drinking gallons of strong tea. The tea and the towel combined are irresistible: the result is always the senior wranglership.

I used to believe in that wet towel and that strong tea. Lord! the things I used to believe when I was young. They would make an Encyclopaedia of Useless Knowledge. I wonder if the author of the popular novel has ever tried working with a wet towel round his or her head: I have. It is difficult enough to move a yard, balancing a dry towel. A heathen Turk may have it in his blood to do so: the ordinary Christian has not got the trick of it. To carry about a wet towel twisted round one's head needs a trained acrobat. Every few minutes the wretched thing works loose. In darkness and in misery, you struggle to get your head out of a clammy towel that clings to you almost with passion. Brain power is wasted in inventing names for that towel—names expressive of your feelings with regard to it. Further time is taken up before the glass, fixing the thing afresh.

You return to your books in the wrong temper, the water trickles down your nose, runs in rivulets down your back. Until you have finally flung the towel out of the window and rubbed yourself dry, work is impossible. The strong tea always gave me indigestion, and made me sleepy. Until I had got over the effects of the tea, attempts at study were useless.

[Because he's so damned clever.]

But the thing that still irritates me most against the hero of the

Jerome K. Jerome

popular novel is the ease with which he learns a modern foreign language. Were he a German waiter, a Swiss barber, or a Polish photographer, I would not envy him; these people do not have to learn a language. My idea is that they boil down a dictionary, and take two table-spoonsful each night before going to bed. By the time the bottle is finished they have the language well into their system. But he is not. He is just an ordinary Anglo-Saxon, and I don't believe in him. I walk about for years with dictionaries in my pocket. Weird-looking ladies and gentlemen gesticulate and rave at me for months. I hide myself in lonely places, repeating idioms to myself out loud, in the hope that by this means they will come readily to me if ever I want them, which I never do. And, after all this, I don't seem to know very much. This irritating ass, who has never left his native suburb, suddenly makes up his mind to travel on the Continent. I find him in the next chapter engaged in complicated psychological argument with French or German savants. It appears—the author had forgotten to mention it before—that one summer a French, or German, or Italian refugee, as the case may happen to be, came to live in the hero's street: thus it is that the hero is able to talk fluently in the native language of that unhappy refugee.

I remember a melodrama visiting a country town where I was staying. The heroine and child were sleeping peacefully in the customary attic. For some reason not quite clear to me, the villain had set fire to the house. He had been complaining through the three preceding acts of the heroine's coldness; maybe it was with some idea of warming her. Escape by way of the staircase was impossible. Each time the poor girl opened the door a flame came in and nearly burned her hair off. It seemed to have been waiting for her.

"Thank God!" said the lady, hastily wrapping the child in a sheet, "that I was brought up a wire walker."

Without a moment's hesitation she opened the attic window and took the nearest telegraph wire to the opposite side of the street.

In the same way, apparently, the hero of the popular novel, finding himself stranded in a foreign land, suddenly recollects that once upon a time he met a refugee, and at once begins to talk. I have met refugees myself. The only thing they have ever taught me is not to leave my brandy flask about.

[And, finally, because I don't believe he's true.]

I don't believe in these heroes and heroines that cannot keep quiet in a foreign language they have taught themselves in an old-world library. My fixed idea is that they muddle along like the rest of us, surprised that so few people understand them, begging everyone they meet not to talk so quickly. These brilliant conversations with foreign philosophers! These passionate interviews with foreign countesses! They fancy they have had them.

I crossed once with an English lady from Boulogne to Folkestone. At Folkestone a little French girl—anxious about her train—asked us a simple question. My companion replied to it with an ease that astonished herself. The little French girl vanished; my companion sighed.

"It's so odd," said my companion, "but I seem to know quite a lot of French the moment I get back to England."

# CHAPTER XIII

[How to be Healthy and Unhappy.]

"They do say," remarked Mrs. Wilkins, as she took the cover off the dish and gave a finishing polish to my plate with the cleanest corner of her apron, "that 'addicks, leastways in May, ain't, strictly speaking, the safest of food. But then, if you listen to all they say, it seems to me, we'd have to give up victuals altogether."

"The haddock, Mrs. Wilkins," I replied, "is a savoury and nourishing dish, the 'poor man's steak' I believe it is commonly called. When I was younger, Mrs. Wilkins, they were cheaper. For twopence one could secure a small specimen, for fourpence one of generous proportions. In the halcyon days of youth, when one's lexicon contained not the word failure (it has crept into later editions, Mrs. Wilkins, the word it was found was occasionally needful), the haddock was of much comfort and support to me, a very present help in time of trouble. In those days a kind friend, without intending it, nearly brought about my death by slow starvation. I had left my umbrella in an omnibus, and the season was rainy. The kind rich friend gave me a new umbrella; it was a rich man's umbrella; we made an ill-assorted pair. Its handle was of ivory, imposing in appearance, ornamented with a golden snake.

[The unsympathetic Umbrella.]

"Following my own judgment I should have pawned that

umbrella, purchased one more suited to my state in life, and 'blued' the difference. But I was fearful of offending my one respectable acquaintance, and for weeks struggled on, hampered by this plutocratic appendage. The humble haddock was denied to me. Tied to this imposing umbrella, how could I haggle with fishmongers for haddocks. At first sight of me—or, rather, of my umbrella—they flew to icy cellars, brought up for my inspection soles at eighteenpence a pound, recommended me prime parts of salmon, which my landlady would have fried in a pan reeking with the mixed remains of pork chops, rashers of bacon and cheese. It was closed to me, the humble coffee shop, where for threepence I could have strengthened my soul with half a pint of cocoa and four "doorsteps"—satisfactory slices of bread smeared with a yellow grease that before the days of County Council inspectors they called butter. You know of them, Mrs. Wilkins? At sight of such nowadays I should turn up my jaded nose. But those were the days of my youth, Mrs. Wilkins. The scent of a thousand hopes was in my nostrils: so they smelt good to me. The fourpenny beefsteak pie, satisfying to the verge of repletion; the succulent saveloy, were not for the owner of the ivory-handled umbrella. On Mondays and Tuesdays, perhaps, I could enjoy life at the rate of five hundred a year—clean serviette a penny extra, and twopence to the waiter, whose income must have been at least four times my own. But from Wednesday to Saturday I had to wander in the wilderness of back streets and silent squares dinnerless, where there were not even to be found locusts and wild honey.

"It was, as I have said, a rainy season, and an umbrella of some sort was a necessity. Fortunately—or I might not be sitting here, Mrs. Wilkins, talking to you now—my one respectable acquaintance was called away to foreign lands, and that umbrella I promptly put 'up the spout.' You understand me?"

Mrs. Wilkins admitted she did, but was of opinion that twenty-five per cent., to say nothing of the halfpenny for the ticket every time, was a wicked imposition.

Jerome K. Jerome

"It did not trouble me, Mrs. Wilkins," I replied, "in this particular instance. It was my determination never to see that umbrella again. The young man behind the counter seemed suspicious, and asked where I got it from. I told him that a friend had given it to me."

"Did he know that he had given it to you?" demanded the young man.

"Upon which I gave him a piece of my mind concerning the character of those who think evil of others, and he gave me five and six, and said he should know me again; and I purchased an umbrella suited to my rank and station, and as fine a haddock as I have ever tasted with the balance, which was sevenpence, for I was feeling hungry.

"The haddock is an excellent fish, Mrs. Wilkins," I said, "and if, as you observe, we listened to all that was said we'd be hungrier at forty, with a balance to our credit at the bank, than ever we were at twenty, with 'no effects' beyond a sound digestion."

[A Martyr to Health.]

"There was a gent in Middle Temple Lane," said Mrs. Wilkins, "as I used to do for. It's my belief as 'e killed 'imself worrying twenty-four hours a day over what 'e called 'is 'ygiene. Leastways 'e's dead and buried now, which must be a comfort to 'imself, feeling as at last 'e's out of danger. All 'is time 'e spent taking care of 'imself—didn't seem to 'ave a leisure moment in which to live. For 'alf an hour every morning 'e'd lie on 'is back on the floor, which is a draughty place, I always 'old, at the best of times, with nothing on but 'is pyjamas, waving 'is arms and legs about, and twisting 'imself into shapes unnatural to a Christian. Then 'e found out that everything 'e'd been doing on 'is back was just all wrong, so 'e turned over and did tricks on 'is stomach—begging your pardon for using the word—that you'd 'ave thought more fit and proper to a worm than to a man. Then all that was discovered to be a mistake. There don't seem nothing certain in these matters. That's the awkward part of it, so it seems to me. 'E got 'imself a machine, by means of which 'e'd 'ang 'imself up to the wall, and behave for all the world like a beetle with a pin stuck through 'im, poor thing. It used to give me the shudders to catch sight of 'im through the 'alf- open door. For that was part of the game: you 'ad to 'ave a current of air through the room, the result of which was that for six months out of the year 'e'd be coughing and blowing 'is nose from morning to night. It was the new treatment, so 'e'd explain to me. You got yourself accustomed to draughts so that they didn't 'urt you, and if you died in the process that only proved that you never ought to 'ave been born.

"Then there came in this new Japanese business, and 'e'd 'ire a little smiling 'eathen to chuck 'im about 'is room for 'alf an hour every morning after breakfast. It got on my nerves after a while 'earing 'im being bumped on the floor every minute, or flung with 'is 'ead into the fire-place. But 'e always said it was doing 'im good. 'E'd argue that it freshened up 'is liver. It was 'is liver that 'e seemed to live for—didn't appear to 'ave any other interest in life. It was the same with 'is food. One year it would be nothing but meat, and next door to raw at that. One of them medical papers 'ad suddenly discovered that we were intended to be a sort of wild beast. The wonder to me is that 'e didn't go out 'unting chickens with a club, and bring 'em 'ome and eat 'em on the mat without any further fuss. For drink it would be boiling water that burnt my fingers merely 'andling the glass. Then some other crank came out with the information that every other crank was wrong—which, taken by itself, sounds natural enough—that meat was fatal to the 'uman system. Upon that 'e becomes all at once a raging, tearing vegetarian, and trouble enough I 'ad learning twenty different ways of cooking beans, which didn't make, so far as I could ever see, the slightest difference— beans they were, and beans they tasted like, whether you called them ragout a la maison, or cutlets a la Pompadour. But it seemed to please 'im.

[He was never pig-headed.]

"Then vegetarianism turned out to be the mistake of our lives. It seemed we made an error giving up monkeys' food. That was our natural victuals; nuts with occasional bananas. As I used to tell 'im, if that was so, then for all we 'ad got out of it we might just as well have stopped up a tree—saved rent and shoe leather. But 'e was one of that sort that don't seem able to 'elp believing everything they read in print. If one of those papers 'ad told 'im to live on the shells and throw away the nuts, 'e'd have made a conscientious endeavour to do so, contending that 'is failure to digest them was merely the result of vicious training—didn't seem to 'ave any likes or dislikes of 'is own. You might 'ave thought 'e was just a bit of public property made to be experimented upon.

"One of the daily papers interviewed an old gent, as said 'e was a 'undred, and I will say from 'is picture as any'ow 'e looked it. 'E said it was all the result of never 'aving swallowed anything 'ot, upon which my gentleman for a week lives on cold porridge, if you'll believe me; although myself I'd rather 'ave died at fifty and got it over. Then another paper dug up from somewhere a sort of animated corpse that said was a 'undred and two, and attributed the unfortunate fact to 'is always 'aving 'ad 'is food as 'ot as 'e could swallow it. A bit of sense did begin to dawn upon 'im then, but too late in the day, I take it. 'E'd played about with 'imself too long. 'E died at thirty-two, looking to all appearance sixty, and you can't say as 'ow it was the result of not taking advice."

[Only just in time.]

"On this subject of health we are much too ready to follow advice," I agreed. "A cousin of mine, Mrs. Wilkins, had a wife who suffered occasionally from headache. No medicine relieved her of them—not altogether. And one day by chance she met a friend who said: 'Come straight with me to Dr. Blank,' who happened to be a specialist famous for having invented a new disease that nobody until the year before had ever heard of. She accompanied her friend to Dr. Blank, and in less than ten minutes he had persuaded her that she had got this new disease, and got it badly; and that her only chance was to let him cut her open and have it out. She was a tolerably healthy woman, with the exception of these occasional headaches, but from what that specialist said it was doubtful whether she would get home alive, unless she let him operate on her then and there, and her friend, who appeared delighted, urged her not to commit suicide, as it were, by missing her turn.

"The result was she consented, and afterwards went home in a four-wheeled cab, and put herself to bed. Her husband, when he returned in the evening and was told, was furious. He said it was all humbug, and by this time she was ready to agree with him. He put on his hat, and started to give that specialist a bit of his mind. The specialist was out, and he had to bottle up his rage until the morning. By then, his wife now really ill for the first time in her life, his indignation had reached boiling point. He was at that specialist's door at half-past nine o clock. At half-past eleven he came back, also in a four-wheeled cab, and day and night nurses for both of them were wired for. He also, it appeared, had arrived at that specialist's door only just in time.

"There's this appendy—whatever they call it," commented Mrs. Wilkins, "why a dozen years ago one poor creature out of ten thousand may possibly 'ave 'ad something wrong with 'is innards. To-day you ain't 'ardly considered respectable unless you've got it, or 'ave 'ad it. I 'ave no patience with their talk. To listen to some of them you'd think as Nature 'adn't made a man—not yet: would never understand the principle of the thing till some of these young chaps 'ad shown 'er 'ow to do it."

[How to avoid Everything.]

"They have now discovered, Mrs. Wilkins," I said, "the germ of old age. They are going to inoculate us for it in early youth, with the result that the only chance of ever getting rid of our friends will be to give them a motor-car. And maybe it will not do to trust to that for long. They will discover that some men's tendency towards getting themselves into trouble is due to some sort of a germ. The man of the future, Mrs. Wilkins, will be inoculated against all chance of gas explosions, storms at sea, bad oysters, and thin ice. Science may eventually discover the germ prompting to ill-assorted marriages, proneness to invest in the wrong stock, uncontrollable desire to recite poetry at evening parties. Religion, politics, education—all these things are so much wasted energy. To live happy and good for ever and ever, all we have to do is to hunt out these various germs and wring their necks for them—or whatever the proper treatment may be. Heaven, I gather from medical science, is merely a place that is free from germs."

"We talk a lot about it," thought Mrs. Wilkins, "but it does not seem to me that we are very much better off than before we took to worrying ourselves for twenty-four 'ours a day about 'ow we are going to live. Lord! to read the advertisements in the papers you would think as 'ow flesh and blood was never intended to 'ave any natural ills. 'Do you ever 'ave a pain in your back?' because, if so, there's a picture of a kind gent who's willing for one and sixpence halfpenny to take it quite away from you—make you look forward to scrubbing floors, and standing over the wash-tub six 'ours at a stretch like to a beanfeast. 'Do you ever feel as though you don't want to get out of bed in the morning?' that's all to be cured by a bottle of their stuff—or two at the outside. Four children to keep, and a sick 'usband on your 'ands used to get me over it when I was younger. I used to fancy it was just because I was tired.

[The one Cure-All.]

"There's some of them seem to think," continued Mrs. Wilkins, "that if you don't get all you want out of this world, and ain't so 'appy as you've persuaded yourself you ought to be, that it's all because you ain't taking the right medicine. Appears to me there's only one doctor as can do for you, all the others talk as though they could, and 'e only comes to each of us once, and then 'e makes no charge."

# CHAPTER XIV

[Europe and the bright American Girl.]

"How does she do it?"

That is what the European girl wants to know. The American girl! She comes over here, and, as a British matron, reduced to slang by force of indignation, once exclaimed to me: "You'd think the whole blessed show belonged to her." The European girl is hampered by her relatives. She has to account for her father: to explain away, if possible, her grandfather. The American girl sweeps them aside:

"Don't you worry about them," she says to the Lord Chamberlain. "It's awfully good of you, but don't you fuss yourself. I'm looking after my old people. That's my department. What I want you to do is just to listen to what I am saying and then hustle around. I can fill up your time all right by myself."

Her father may be a soap-boiler, her grandmother may have gone out charing.

"That's all right," she says to her Ambassador: "They're not coming. You just take my card and tell the King that when he's got a few minutes to spare I'll be pleased to see him."

And the extraordinary thing is that, a day or two afterwards, the invitation arrives.

A modern writer has said that "I'm Murrican" is the Civis Romanus sum of the present-day woman's world. The late King of Saxony, did, I believe, on one occasion make a feeble protest at being asked to receive the daughter of a retail bootmaker. The young lady, nonplussed for the moment, telegraphed to her father in Detroit. The answer came back next morning: "Can't call it selling—practically giving them away. See Advertisement." The lady was presented as the daughter of an eminent philanthropist.

It is due to her to admit that, taking her as a class, the American girl is a distinct gain to European Society. Her influence is against convention and in favour of simplicity. One of her greatest charms, in the eyes of the European man, is that she listens to him. I cannot say whether it does her any good. Maybe she does not remember it all, but while you are talking she does give you her attention. The English woman does not always. She greets you pleasantly enough:

"I've so often wanted to meet you," she says, "must you really go?"

It strikes you as sudden: you had no intention of going for hours. But the hint is too plain to be ignored. You are preparing to agree that you really must when, looking round, you gather that the last remark was not addressed to you, but to another gentleman who is shaking hands with her:

"Now, perhaps we shall be able to talk for five minutes," she says. "I've so often wanted to say that I shall never forgive you. You have been simply horrid."

Again you are confused, until you jump to the conclusion that the latter portion of the speech is probably intended for quite another party with whom, at the moment, her back towards you, she is engaged in a whispered conversation. When he is gone she turns again to you. But the varied expressions that pass across her face while you are discussing with her the disadvantages of Protection, bewilder you. When, explaining your own difficulty in arriving at a conclusion, you remark that Great Britain is an island, she roguishly shakes her head. It is not that she has forgotten her geography, it is that she is conducting a conversation by signs with a lady at the other end of the room. When you observe that the working classes must be fed, she smiles archly while murmuring:

"Oh, do you really think so?"

You are about to say something strong on the subject of dumping. Apparently she has disappeared. You find that she is reaching round behind you to tap a new arrival with her fan.

[She has the Art of Listening.]

Now, the American girl looks at you, and just listens to you with her eyes fixed on you all the time. You gather that, as far as she is concerned, the rest of the company are passing shadows. She wants to hear what you have to say about Bimetallism: her trouble is lest she may miss a word of it. From a talk with an American girl one comes away with the conviction that one is a brilliant conversationalist, who can hold a charming woman spell-bound. This may not be good for one: but while it lasts, the sensation is pleasant.

Even the American girl cannot, on all occasions, sweep from her path the cobwebs of old-world etiquette. Two American ladies told me a sad tale of things that had happened to them not long ago in Dresden. An officer of rank and standing invited them to breakfast with him on the ice. Dames and nobles of the plus haut ton would be there. It is a social function that occurs every Sunday morning in Dresden during the skating season. The great lake in the Grosser Garten is covered with all sorts and conditions of people. Prince and commoner circle and recircle round one another. But they do not mix. The girls were pleased. They secured the services of an elderly lady, the widow of an analytical chemist: unfortunately, she could not skate. They wrapped her up and put her in a sledge. While they were in the garde robe putting on their skates, a German gentleman came up and bowed to them.

He was a nice young man of prepossessing appearance and amiable manners. They could not call to mind his name, but remembered having met him, somewhere, and on more than one occasion. The American girl is always sociable: they bowed and smiled, and said it was a fine day. He replied with volubility, and helped them down on to the ice. He was really most attentive. They saw their friend, the officer of noble family, and, with the assistance of the German gentleman, skated towards him. He glided past them. They thought that maybe he did not know enough to stop, so they turned and skated after him. They chased him three times round the pond and then, feeling tired, eased up and took counsel together.

"I'm sure he must have seen us," said the younger girl. "What does he mean by it?"

"Well, I have not come down here to play forfeits," said the other, "added to which I want my breakfast. You wait here a minute, I'll go and have it out with him."

He was standing only a dozen yards away. Alone, though not a good performer on the ice, she contrived to cover half the distance dividing them. The officer, perceiving her, came to her assistance and greeted her with effusion.

[The Republican Idea in practice.]

"Oh," said the lady, who was feeling indignant, "I thought maybe you had left your glasses at home."

"I am sorry," said the officer, "but it is impossible."

"What's impossible?" demanded the lady.

"That I can be seen speaking to you," declared the officer, "while you are in company with that—that person."

"What person?" She thought maybe he was alluding to the lady in the sledge. The chaperon was not showy, but, what is better, she was good. And, anyhow, it was the best the girls had been able to do. So far as they were concerned, they had no use for a chaperon. The idea had been a thoughtful concession to European prejudice.

"The person in knickerbockers," explained the officer.

"Oh, THAT," exclaimed the lady, relieved: "he just came up and made himself agreeable while we were putting on our skates. We have met him somewhere, but I can't exactly fix him for the moment."

"You have met him possibly at Wiesman's, in the Pragerstrasse: he is one of the attendants there," said the officer.

The American girl is Republican in her ideas, but she draws the line at hairdressers. In theory it is absurd: the hairdresser is a man and a brother: but we are none of us logical all the way. It made her mad, the thought that she had been seen by all Dresden Society skating with a hairdresser.

"Well," she said, "I do call that impudence. Why, they wouldn't do that even in Chicago."

And she returned to where the hairdresser was illustrating to her friend the Dutch roll, determined to explain to him, as politely as possible, that although the free and enlightened Westerner has abolished social distinctions, he has not yet abolished them to that extent.

Had he been a commonplace German hairdresser he would have understood English, and all might have been easy. But to the "classy" German hairdresser, English is not so necessary, and the American ladies had reached, as regards their German, only the "improving" stage. In her excitement she confused the subjunctive and the imperative, and told him that he "might" go. He had no wish to go; he assured them—so they

Jerome K. Jerome

gathered—that his intention was to devote the morning to their service. He must have been a stupid man, but it is a type occasionally encountered. Two pretty women had greeted his advances with apparent delight. They were Americans, and the American girl was notoriously unconventional. He knew himself to be a good-looking young fellow. It did not occur to him that in expressing willingness to dispense with his attendance they could be in earnest.

There was nothing for it, so it seemed to the girls, but to request the assistance of the officer, who continued to skate round and round them at a distance of about ten yards. So again the elder young lady, seizing her opportunity, made appeal.

[What the Soldier dared not do.]

"I cannot," persisted the officer, who, having been looking forward to a morning with two of the prettiest girls in Dresden, was also feeling mad. "I dare not be seen speaking to a hairdresser. You must get rid of him."

"But we can't," said the girl. "We do not know enough German, and he can't, or he won't, understand us. For goodness sake come and help us. We'll be spending the whole morning with him if you don't."

The German officer said he was desolate. Steps would be taken—later in the week—the result of which would probably be to render that young hairdresser prematurely bald. But, meanwhile, beyond skating round and round them, for which they did not even feel they wanted to thank him, the German officer could do nothing for them. They tried being rude to the hairdresser: he mistook it for American chic. They tried joining hands and running away from him, but they were not good skaters, and he thought they were trying to show him the cake walk. They both fell down and hurt themselves, and it is difficult to be angry with a man, even a hairdresser, when he is doing his best to pick you up and comfort you.

The chaperon was worse than useless. She was very old. She had been promised her breakfast, but saw no signs of it. She could not speak German; and remembered somewhat late in the day that two young ladies had no business to accept breakfast at the hands of German officers: and, if they did, at least they might see that they got it. She appeared to be willing to talk about decadence of modern manners to almost any extent, but the subject of the hairdresser, and how to get rid of him, only bored her.

Their first stroke of luck occurred when the hairdresser, showing them the "dropped three," fell down and temporarily stunned himself. It was not kind of them, but they were desperate. They flew for the bank just anyhow, and, scrambling over the grass, gained the restaurant. The officer, overtaking them at the door, led them to the table that had been reserved for them, then hastened back to hunt for the chaperon. The girls thought their trouble was over. Had they glanced behind them their joy would have been shorter-lived than even was the case. The hairdresser had recovered consciousness in time to see them waddling over the grass. He thought they were running to fetch him brandy. When the officer returned with the chaperon he found the hairdresser sitting opposite to them, explaining that he really was not hurt, and suggesting that, as they were there, perhaps they would like something to eat and drink.

The girls made one last frantic appeal to the man of buckram and pipeclay, but the etiquette of the Saxon Army was inexorable. It transpired that he might kill the hairdresser, but nothing else: he must not speak to him—not even explain to the poor devil why it was that he was being killed.

[Her path of Usefulness.]

It did not seem quite worth it. They had some sandwiches and coffee at the hairdresser's expense, and went home in a cab: while the chaperon had breakfast with the officer of noble family.

The American girl has succeeded in freeing European social intercourse from many of its hide-bound conventions. There is still much work for her to do. But I have faith in her.

# CHAPTER XV

[Music and the Savage.]

I never visit a music-hall without reflecting concerning the great future there must be before the human race.

How young we are, how very young! And think of all we have done! Man is still a mere boy. He has only just within the last half-century been put into trousers. Two thousand years ago he wore long clothes—the Grecian robe, the Roman toga. Then followed the Little Lord Fauntleroy period, when he went about dressed in a velvet suit with lace collar and cuffs, and had his hair curled for him. The late lamented Queen Victoria put him into trousers. What a wonderful little man he will be when he is grown up!

A clergyman friend of mine told me of a German Kurhaus to which he was sent for his sins and his health. It was a resort, for some reason, specially patronized by the more elderly section of the higher English middle class. Bishops were there, suffering from fatty degeneration of the heart caused by too close application to study; ancient spinsters of good family subject to spasms; gouty retired generals. Can anybody tell me how many men in the British Army go to a general? Somebody once assured me it was five thousand, but that is absurd, on the face of it. The British Army, in that case, would have to be counted by millions. There are a goodish few American colonels still knocking about. The American colonel is still to be met with here and there by the curious traveller, but

Jerome K. Jerome

compared with the retired British general he is an extinct species. In Cheltenham and Brighton and other favoured towns there are streets of nothing but retired British generals—squares of retired British generals—whole crescents of British generals. Abroad there are pensions with a special scale of charges for British generals. In Switzerland there has even been talk of reserving railway compartments "For British Generals Only." In Germany, when you do not say distinctly and emphatically on being introduced that you are not a British general, you are assumed, as a matter of course, to be a British general. During the Boer War, when I was residing in a small garrison town on the Rhine, German military men would draw me aside and ask of me my own private personal views as to the conduct of the campaign. I would give them my views freely, explain to them how I would finish the whole thing in a week.

"But how in the face of the enemy's tactics—" one of them would begin.

"Bother the enemy's tactics," I would reply. "Who cares for tactics?"

"But surely a British general—" they would persist. "Who's a British general?" I would retort, "I am talking to you merely as a plain commonsense man, with a head on my shoulders."

They would apologize for their mistake. But this is leading me away from that German Kurhaus.

[Recreation for the Higher clergy.]

My clergyman friend found life there dull. The generals and the spinsters left to themselves might have played cards, but they thought of the poor bishops who would have had to look on envious. The bishops and the spinsters might have sung ballads, but the British general after dinner does not care for ballads, and had mentioned it. The bishops and the generals might have told each other stories, but could not before the ladies. My clergyman friend stood the awful solemnity of three evenings, then cautiously felt his way towards revelry. He started with an intellectual game called "Quotations." You write down quotations on a piece of paper, and the players have to add the author's name. It roped in four old ladies, and the youngest bishop. One or two generals tried a round, but not being familiar with quotations voted the game slow.

The next night my friend tried "Consequences." "Saucy Miss A. met the gay General B. in"—most unlikely places. "He said." Really it was fortunate that General B. remained too engrossed in the day before yesterday's Standard to overhear, or Miss A. could never have again faced him. "And she replied." The suppressed giggles excited the curiosity of the non-players. Most of the bishops and half the generals asked to be allowed to join. The giggles grew into roars. Those standing out found that they could not read their papers in comfort.

From "Consequences" the descent was easy. The tables and chairs were pushed against the walls, the bishops and the spinsters and the generals would sit in a ring upon the floor playing hunt the slipper. Musical chairs made the two hours between bed and dinner the time of the day they all looked forward to: the steady trot with every nerve alert, the ear listening for the sudden stoppage of the music, the eye seeking with artfulness the likeliest chair, the volcanic silence, the mad scramble.

The generals felt themselves fighting their battles over again, the spinsters blushed and preened themselves, the bishops took interest in proving that even the Church could be prompt of decision and swift of movement. Before the week was out they were playing Puss-in-the- corner; ladies feeling young again were archly beckoning to stout deans, to whom were returning all the sensations of a curate. The swiftness with which the gouty generals found they could still hobble surprised even themselves.

[Why are we so young?]

But it is in the music-hall, as I have said, that I am most impressed with the youthfulness of man. How delighted we are when the long man in the little boy's hat, having asked his short brother a riddle, and before he can find time to answer it, hits him over the stomach with an umbrella! How we clap our hands and shout with glee! It isn't really his stomach: it is a bolster tied round his waist—we know that; but seeing the long man whack at that bolster with an umbrella gives us almost as much joy as if the bolster were not there.

I laugh at the knockabout brothers, I confess, so long as they are on the stage; but they do not convince me. Reflecting on the performance afterwards, my dramatic sense revolts against the "plot." I cannot accept the theory of their being brothers. The difference in size alone is a strain upon my imagination. It is not probable that of two children of the same parents one should measure six foot six, and the other five foot four. Even allowing for a freak of nature, and accepting the fact that they might be brothers, I do not believe they would remain so inseparable. The short brother would have succeeded before now in losing the long brother. Those continual bangings over the head and stomach would have weakened whatever affection the short brother might originally have felt towards his long relation. At least, he would insist upon the umbrella being left at home.

"I will go for a walk with you," he might say, "I will stand stock still with you in Trafalgar Square in the midst of the traffic while you ask me silly riddles, but not if you persist in bringing with you that absurd umbrella. You are too handy with it. Put it back in the rack before we start, or go out by yourself."

Besides, my sense of justice is outraged. Why should the short brother be banged and thumped without reason? The Greek dramatist would have explained to us that the shorter brother had committed a crime against the gods. Aristophanes would have made the longer brother the instrument of the Furies. The riddles he asked would have had bearing upon the shorter brother's sin. In this way the spectator would have enjoyed amusement combined with the satisfactory sense that Nemesis is ever present in human affairs. I present the idea, for what it may be worth, to the concoctors of knockabout turns.

[Where Brotherly (and Sisterly) Love reigns supreme]

The family tie is always strong on the music-hall stage. The acrobatic troupe is always a "Family": Pa, Ma, eight brothers and sisters, and the baby. A more affectionate family one rarely sees. Pa and Ma are a trifle stout, but still active. Baby, dear little fellow, is full of humour. Ladies do not care to go on the music- hall stage unless they can take their sister with them. I have seen a performance given by eleven sisters, all the same size and apparently all the same age. She must have been a wonderful woman—the mother. They all had golden hair, and all wore precisely similar frocks—a charming but decolletee arrangement—in claret-coloured velvet over blue silk stockings. So far as I could gather, they all had the same young man. No doubt he found it difficult amongst them to make up his mind.

"Arrange it among yourselves," he no doubt had said, "it is quite immaterial to me. You are so much alike, it is impossible that a fellow loving one should not love the lot of you. So long as I marry into the family I really don't care."

When a performer appears alone on the music-hall stage it is easy to understand why. His or her domestic life has been a failure. I listened one evening to six songs in succession. The first two were sung by a gentleman. He entered with his clothes hanging upon him in shreds. He explained that he had just come from an argument with his wife. He showed us the brick with which she had hit him, and the bump at the back of his head that had resulted. The funny man's marriage is never a success. But really this seems to be his own fault. "She was such a lovely girl," he tells us, "with a face—well, you'd hardly call it a face, it was more like a gas explosion. Then she had those wonderful sort of eyes that you can see two ways at once

Jerome K. Jerome

with, one of them looks down the street, while the other one is watching round the corner. Can see you coming any way. And her mouth!"

It appears that if she stands anywhere near the curb and smiles, careless people mistake her for a pillar-box, and drop letters into her.

"And such a voice!" We are told it is a perfect imitation of a motor-car. When she laughs people spring into doorways to escape being run over.

If he will marry that sort of woman, what can he expect? The man is asking for it.

The lady who followed him also told us a sad story of mis-placed trust. She also was comic—so the programme assured us. The humorist appears to have no luck. She had lent her lover money to buy the ring, and the licence, and to furnish the flat. He did buy the ring, and he furnished the flat, but it was for another lady. The audience roared. I have heard it so often asked, "What is humour?" From observation, I should describe it as other people's troubles.

A male performer followed her. He came on dressed in a night-shirt, carrying a baby. His wife, it seemed, had gone out for the evening with the lodger. That was his joke. It was the most successful song of the whole six.

[The one sure Joke.]

A philosopher has put it on record that he always felt sad when he reflected on the sorrows of humanity. But when he reflected on its amusements he felt sadder still.

Why was it so funny that the baby had the lodger's nose? We laughed for a full minute by the clock.

Why do I love to see a flabby-faced man go behind curtains,

and, emerging in a wig and a false beard, say that he is now Bismarck or Mr. Chamberlain? I have felt resentment against the Lightning Impersonator ever since the days of Queen Victoria's Diamond Jubilee. During that summer every Lightning Impersonator ended his show by shouting, while the band played the National Anthem, "Queen Victoria!" He was not a bit like Queen Victoria. He did not even, to my thinking, look a lady; but at once I had to stand up in my place and sing "God save the Queen." It was a time of enthusiastic loyalty; if you did not spring up quickly some patriotic old fool from the back would reach across and hit you over the head with the first thing he could lay his hands upon.

Other music-hall performers caught at the idea. By ending up with "God save the Queen" any performer, however poor, could retire in a whirlwind of applause. Niggers, having bored us with tiresome songs about coons and honeys and Swanee Rivers, would, as a last resource, strike up "God save the Queen" on the banjo. The whole house would have to rise and cheer. Elderly Sisters Trippet, having failed to arouse our enthusiasm by allowing us a brief glimpse of an ankle, would put aside all frivolity, and tell us of a hero lover named George, who had fought somebody somewhere for his Queen and country. "He fell!"—bang from the big drum and blue limelight. In a recumbent position he appears to have immediately started singing "God save the Queen."

[How Anarchists are made.]

Sleepy members of the audience would be hastily awakened by their friends. We would stagger to our feet. The Sisters Trippet, with eyes fixed on the chandelier, would lead us: to the best of our ability we would sing "God save the Queen."

There have been evenings when I have sung "God save the Queen" six times. Another season of it, and I should have become a Republican.

The singer of patriotic songs is generally a stout and puffy man. The perspiration pours from his face as the result of the violent gesticulations with which he tells us how he stormed the fort. He must have reached it very hot.

"There were ten to one agin us, boys." We feel that this was a miscalculation on the enemy's part. Ten to one "agin" such wildly gesticulating Britishers was inviting defeat.

It seems to have been a terrible battle notwithstanding. He shows us with a real sword how it was done. Nothing could have lived within a dozen yards of that sword. The conductor of the orchestra looks nervous. Our fear is lest he will end by cutting off his own head. His recollections are carrying him away. Then follows "Victory!"

The gas men and the programme sellers cheer wildly. We conclude with the inevitable "God save the King."

# CHAPTER XVI

[The Ghost and the Blind Children.]

Ghosts are in the air. It is difficult at this moment to avoid talking of ghosts. The first question you are asked on being introduced this season is:

"Do you believe in ghosts?"

I would be so glad to believe in ghosts. This world is much too small for me. Up to a century or two ago the intellectual young man found it sufficient for his purposes. It still contained the unknown—the possible—within its boundaries. New continents were still to be discovered: we dreamt of giants, Liliputians, desert-fenced Utopias. We set our sail, and Wonderland lay ever just beyond our horizon. To-day the world is small, the light railway runs through the desert, the coasting steamer calls at the Islands of the Blessed, the last mystery has been unveiled, the fairies are dead, the talking birds are silent. Our baffled curiosity turns for relief outwards. We call upon the dead to rescue us from our monotony. The first authentic ghost will be welcomed as the saviour of humanity.

But he must be a living ghost—a ghost we can respect, a ghost we can listen to. The poor spiritless addle-headed ghost that has hitherto haunted our blue chambers is of no use to us. I remember a thoughtful man once remarking during argument that if he believed in ghosts—the silly, childish spooks about

Jerome K. Jerome

which we had been telling anecdotes—death would possess for him an added fear: the idea that his next dwelling-place would be among such a pack of dismal idiots would sadden his departing hours. What was he to talk to them about? Apparently their only interest lay in recalling their earthly troubles. The ghost of the lady unhappily married who had been poisoned, or had her throat cut, who every night for the last five hundred years had visited the chamber where it happened for no other purpose than to scream about it! what a tiresome person she would be to meet! All her conversation during the long days would be around her earthly wrongs. The other ghosts, in all probability, would have heard about that husband of hers, what he said, and what he did, till they were sick of the subject. A newcomer would be seized upon with avidity.

A lady of repute writes to a magazine that she once occupied for a season a wainscotted room in an old manor house. On several occasions she awoke in the night: each time to witness the same ghostly performance. Four gentlemen sat round a table playing cards. Suddenly one of them sprang to his feet and plunged a dagger into the back of his partner. The lady does not say so: one presumes it was his partner. I have, myself, when playing bridge, seen an expression on my partner's face that said quite plainly:

"I would like to murder you."

I have not the memory for bridge. I forget who it was that, last trick but seven, played the two of clubs. I thought it was he, my partner. I thought it meant that I was to take an early opportunity of forcing trumps. I don't know why I thought so, I try to explain why I thought so. It sounds a silly argument even to myself; I feel I have not got it quite right. Added to which it was not my partner who played the two of clubs, it was Dummy. If I had only remembered this, and had concluded from it—as I ought to have done—that my partner had the ace of diamonds—as otherwise why did he pass my knave?—we might have saved the odd trick. I have not the head for bridge. It is only an ordinary head—mine. I have no business to play bridge.

[Why not, occasionally, a cheerful Ghost.]

But to return to our ghosts. These four gentlemen must now and again, during their earthly existence, have sat down to a merry game of cards. There must have been evenings when nobody was stabbed. Why choose an unpleasant occasion to harp exclusively upon it? Why do ghosts never give a cheerful show? The lady who was poisoned! there must have been other evenings in her life. Why does she not show us "The first meeting": when he gave her the violets and said they were like her eyes? He wasn't always poisoning her. There must have been a period before he ever thought of poisoning her. Cannot these ghosts do something occasionally in what is termed "the lighter vein"? If they haunt a forest glade, it is to perform a duel to the death, or an assassination. Why cannot they, for a change, give us an old-time picnic, or "The hawking party," which, in Elizabethan costume, should make a pretty picture? Ghostland would appear to be obsessed by the spirit of the Scandinavian drama: murders, suicides, ruined fortunes, and broken hearts are the only material made use of. Why is not a dead humorist allowed now and then to write the sketch? There must be plenty of dead comic lovers; why are they never allowed to give a performance?

[Where are the dead Humorists?]

A cheerful person contemplates death with alarm. What is he to do in this land of ghosts? there is no place for him. Imagine the commonplace liver of a humdrum existence being received into ghostland. He enters nervous, shy, feeling again the new boy at school. The old ghosts gather round him.

"How do you come here—murdered?"

"No, at least, I don't think so."

Jerome K. Jerome

"Suicide?

"No—can't remember the name of it now. Began with a chill on the liver, I think."

The ghosts are disappointed. But a happy suggestion is made. Perhaps he was the murderer; that would be even better. Let him think carefully; can he recollect ever having committed a murder? He racks his brains in vain, not a single murder comes to his recollection. He never forged a will. Doesn't even know where anything is hid. Of what use will he be in ghostland? One pictures him passing the centuries among a moody crowd of uninteresting mediocrities, brooding perpetually over their wasted lives. Only the ghosts of ladies and gentlemen mixed up in crime have any "show" in ghostland.

[The Spirit does not shine as a Conversationalist.]

I feel an equal dissatisfaction with the spirits who are supposed to return to us and communicate with us through the medium of three-legged tables. I do not deny the possibility that spirits exist. I am even willing to allow them their three-legged tables. It must be confessed it is a clumsy method. One cannot help regretting that during all the ages they have not evolved a more dignified system. One feels that the three-legged table must hamper them. One can imagine an impatient spirit getting tired of spelling out a lengthy story on a three-legged table. But, as I have said, I am willing to assume that, for some spiritual reason unfathomable to my mere human intelligence, that three-legged table is essential. I am willing also to accept the human medium. She is generally an unprepossessing lady running somewhat to bulk. If a gentleman, he so often has dirty finger-nails, and smells of stale beer. I think myself it would be so much simpler if the spirit would talk to me direct; we could get on quicker. But there is that about the medium, I am told, which appeals to a spirit. Well, it is his affair, not mine, and I waive the argument. My real stumbling-block is the spirit himself—the sort of conversation that, when he does talk, he indulges in. I cannot help feeling that his conversation is not worth the paraphernalia. I can talk better than that myself.

The late Professor Huxley, who took some trouble over this matter, attended some half-dozen seances, and then determined to attend no more.

"I have," he said, "for my sins to submit occasionally to the society of live bores. I refuse to go out of my way to spend an evening in the dark with dead bores."

The spiritualists themselves admit that their table-rapping spooks are precious dull dogs; it would be difficult, in face of the communications recorded, for them to deny it. They explain to us that they have not yet achieved communication with the higher spiritual Intelligences. The more intelligent spirits—for some reason that the spiritualists themselves are unable to explain—do not want to talk to them, appear to have something else to do. At present—so I am told, and can believe—it is only the spirits of lower intelligence that care to turn up on these evenings. The spiritualists argue that, by continuing, the higher-class spirits will later on be induced to "come in." I fail to follow the argument. It seems to me that we are frightening them away. Anyhow, myself I shall wait awhile.

When the spirit comes along that can talk sense, that can tell me something I don't know, I shall be glad to meet him. The class of spirit that we are getting just at present does not appeal to me. The thought of him—the reflection that I shall die and spend the rest of eternity in his company—does not comfort me.

[She is now a Believer.]

A lady of my acquaintance tells me it is marvellous how much these spirits seem to know. On her very first visit, the spirit, through the voice of the medium—an elderly gentleman residing obscurely in Clerkenwell—informed her without a moment's hesitation that she possessed a relative with the Christian name of George. (I am not making this up—it is real.) This gave her at first the idea that spiritualism was a fraud. She had no relative named George—at least, so she thought. But a morning or two later her husband received a letter from Australia. "By Jove!" he exclaimed, as he glanced at the last page, "I had forgotten all about the poor old beggar."

"Whom is it from?" she asked.

"Oh, nobody you know—haven't seen him myself for twenty years—a third or fourth cousin of mine—George—"

She never heard the surname, she was too excited. The spirit had been right from the beginning; she HAD a relative named George. Her faith in spiritualism is now as a rock.

There are thousands of folk who believe in Old Moore's Almanac. My difficulty would be not to believe in the old gentleman. I see that for the month of January last he foretold us that the Government would meet with determined and persistent opposition. He warned us that there would be much sickness about, and that rheumatism would discover its old victims. How does he know these things? Is it that the stars really do communicate with him, or does he "feel it in his bones," as the saying is up North?

During February, he mentioned, the weather would be unsettled. He concluded:

"The word Taxation will have a terrible significance for both Government and people this month."

Really, it is quite uncanny. In March:

"Theatres will do badly during the month."

There seems to be no keeping anything from Old Moore. In April "much dissatisfaction will be expressed among Post

Office employees." That sounds probable, on the face of it. In any event, I will answer for our local postman.

In May "a wealthy magnate is going to die." In June there is going to be a fire. In July "Old Moore has reason to fear there will be trouble."

I do hope he may be wrong, and yet somehow I feel a conviction that he won't be. Anyhow, one is glad it has been put off till July.

In August "one in high authority will be in danger of demise." In September "zeal" on the part of persons mentioned "will outstrip discretion." In October Old Moore is afraid again. He cannot avoid a haunting suspicion that "Certain people will be victimized by extensive fraudulent proceedings."

In November "the public Press will have its columns full of important news." The weather will be "adverse," and "a death will occur in high circles." This makes the second in one year. I am glad I do not belong to the higher circles.

[How does he do it?]

In December Old Moore again foresees trouble, just when I was hoping it was all over. "Frauds will come to light, and death will find its victims."

And all this information is given to us for a penny.

The palmist examines our hand. "You will go a journey," he tells us. It is marvellous! How could he have known that only the night before we had been discussing the advisability of taking the children to Margate for the holidays?

"There is trouble in store for you," he tells us, regretfully, "but you will get over it." We feel that the future has no secret hidden from him.

We have "presentiments" that people we love, who are climbing mountains, who are fond of ballooning, are in danger.

The sister of a friend of mine who went out to the South African War as a volunteer had three presentiments of his death. He came home safe and sound, but admitted that on three distinct occasions he had been in imminent danger. It seemed to the dear lady a proof of everything she had ever read.

Another friend of mine was waked in the middle of the night by his wife, who insisted that he should dress himself and walk three miles across a moor because she had had a dream that something terrible was happening to a bosom friend of hers. The bosom friend and her husband were rather indignant at being waked at two o'clock in the morning, but their indignation was mild compared with that of the dreamer on learning that nothing was the matter. From that day forward a coldness sprang up between the two families.

I would give much to believe in ghosts. The interest of life would be multiplied by its own square power could we communicate with the myriad dead watching us from their mountain summits. Mr. Zangwill, in a poem that should live, draws for us a pathetic picture of blind children playing in a garden, laughing, romping. All their lives they have lived in darkness; they are content. But, the wonder of it, could their eyes by some miracle be opened!

[Blind Children playing in a World of Darkness.]

May not we be but blind children, suggests the poet, living in a world of darkness—laughing, weeping, loving, dying— knowing nothing of the wonder round us?

The ghosts about us, with their god-like faces, it might be good to look at them.

But these poor, pale-faced spooks, these dull-witted, table-thumping spirits: it would be sad to think that of such was the kingdom of the Dead.

# CHAPTER XVII

[Parents and their Teachers.]

My heart has been much torn of late, reading of the wrongs of Children. It has lately been discovered that Children are being hampered and harassed in their career by certain brutal and ignorant persons called, for want of a better name, parents. The parent is a selfish wretch who, out of pure devilment, and without consulting the Child itself upon the subject, lures innocent Children into the world, apparently for the purpose merely of annoying them. The parent does not understand the Child when he has got it; he does not understand anything, not much. The only person who understands the Child is the young gentleman fresh from College and the elderly maiden lady, who, between them, produce most of the literature that explains to us the Child.

The parent does not even know how to dress the Child. The parent will persist in dressing the Child in a long and trailing garment that prevents the Child from kicking. The young gentleman fresh from College grows almost poetical in his contempt. It appears that the one thing essential for the health of a young child is that it should have perfect freedom to kick. Later on the parent dresses the Child in short clothes, and leaves bits of its leg bare. The elderly maiden Understander of Children, quoting medical opinion, denounces us as criminals for leaving any portion of that precious leg uncovered. It appears that the partially uncovered leg of childhood is responsible for most of the disease that flesh is heir to.

Then we put it into boots. We "crush its delicately fashioned feet into hideous leather instruments of torture." That is the sort of phrase that is hurled at us! The picture conjured up is that of some fiend in human shape, calling itself a father, seizing some helpless cherub by the hair, and, while drowning its pathetic wails for mercy beneath roars of demon laughter, proceeding to bind about its tender bones some ancient curiosity dug from the dungeons of the Inquisition.

If the young gentleman fresh from College or the maiden lady Understander could be, if only for a month or two, a father! If only he or she could guess how gladly the father of limited income would reply,

"My dear, you are wrong in saying that the children must have boots. That is an exploded theory. The children must not have boots. I refuse to be a party to crushing their delicately fashioned feet into hideous leather instruments of torture. The young gentleman fresh from College and the elderly maiden Understander have decided that the children must not have boots. Do not let me hear again that out- of-date word—boots."

If there were only one young gentleman fresh from College, one maiden lady Understander teaching us our duty, life would be simpler. But there are so many young gentlemen from College, so many maiden lady Understanders, on the job—if I may be permitted a vulgarism; and as yet they are not all agreed. It is distracting for the parent anxious to do right. We put the little dears into sandals, and then at once other young gentlemen from College, other maiden lady Understanders, point to us as would-be murderers. Long clothes are fatal, short clothes are deadly, boots are instruments of torture, to allow children to go about with bare feet shows that we regard them as Incumbrances, and, with low cunning, are seeking to be rid of them.

[Their first attempt.]

I knew a pair of parents. I am convinced, in spite of all that can be said to the contrary, they were fond of their Child; it was their first. They were anxious to do the right thing. They read with avidity all books and articles written on the subject of Children. They read that a Child should always sleep lying on its back, and took it in turns to sit awake o' nights to make sure that the Child was always right side up.

But another magazine told them that Children allowed to sleep lying on their backs grew up to be idiots. They were sad they had not read of this before, and started the Child on its right side. The Child, on the contrary, appeared to have a predilection for the left, the result being that neither the parents nor the baby itself for the next three weeks got any sleep worth speaking of.

Later on, by good fortune, they came across a treatise that said a Child should always be allowed to choose its own position while sleeping, and their friends persuaded them to stop at that—told them they would never strike a better article if they searched the whole British Museum Library. It troubled them to find that Child sometimes sleeping curled up with its toe in its mouth, and sometimes flat on its stomach with its head underneath the pillow. But its health and temper were decidedly improved.

[The Parent can do no right.]

There is nothing the parent can do right. You would think that now and then he might, if only by mere accident, blunder into sense. But, no, there seems to be a law against it. He brings home woolly rabbits and indiarubber elephants, and expects the Child to be contented "forsooth" with suchlike aids to its education. As a matter of fact, the Child is content: it bangs its own head with the woolly rabbit and does itself no harm; it tries to swallow the indiarubber elephant; it does not succeed, but continues to hope. With that woolly rabbit and that indiarubber elephant it would be as happy as the day is long if only the young gentleman from Cambridge would leave it alone, and not put new ideas into its head. But the gentleman from Cambridge and the maiden lady Understander are convinced that the future of the race depends upon leaving the Child untrammelled to select its own amusements. A friend of mine, during his wife's absence once on a visit to her mother, tried the experiment.

The Child selected a frying-pan. How it got the frying-pan remains to this day a mystery. The cook said "frying-pans don't walk upstairs." The nurse said she should be sorry to call anyone a liar, but that there was commonsense in everything. The scullery-maid said that if everybody did their own work other people would not be driven beyond the limits of human endurance; and the housekeeper said that she was sick and tired of life. My friend said it did not matter. The Child clung to the frying-pan with passion. The book my friend was reading said that was how the human mind was formed: the Child's instinct prompted it to seize upon objects tending to develop its brain faculty. What the parent had got to do was to stand aside and watch events.

The Child proceeded to black everything about the nursery with the bottom of the frying-pan. It then set to work to lick the frying-pan clean. The nurse, a woman of narrow ideas, had a presentiment that later on it would be ill. My friend explained to her the error the world had hitherto committed: it had imagined that the parent knew a thing or two that the Child didn't. In future the Children were to do their bringing up themselves. In the house of the future the parents would be allotted the attics where they would be out of the way. They might occasionally be allowed down to dinner, say, on Sundays.

The Child, having exhausted all the nourishment the frying-pan contained, sought to develop its brain faculty by thumping itself over the head with the flat of the thing. With the selfishness of the average parent—thinking chiefly of what the Coroner might say, and indifferent to the future of humanity, my friend insisted upon changing the game.

[His foolish talk.]

The parent does not even know how to talk to his own Child. The Child is yearning to acquire a correct and dignified mode of expression. The parent says: "Did ums. Did naughty table hurt ickle tootsie pootsies? Baby say: "Oo naughty table. Me no love 'oo.'"

The Child despairs of ever learning English. What should we think ourselves were we to join a French class, and were the Instructor to commence talking to us French of this description? What the Child, according to the gentleman from Cambridge, says to itself is,

"Oh for one hour's intelligent conversation with a human being who can talk the language."

Will not the young gentleman from Cambridge descend to detail? Will he not give us a specimen dialogue?

A celebrated lady writer, who has made herself the mouthpiece of feminine indignation against male stupidity, took up the cudgels a little while ago on behalf of Mrs. Caudle. She admitted Mrs. Caudle appeared to be a somewhat foolish lady. "BUT WHAT HAD CAUDLE EVER DONE TO IMPROVE MRS. CAUDLE'S MIND?" Had he ever sought, with intelligent illuminating conversation, to direct her thoughts towards other topics than lent umbrellas and red-headed minxes?

It is my complaint against so many of our teachers. They scold us for what we do, but so rarely tell us what we ought to do. Tell me how to talk to my baby, and I am willing to try. It is not as if I took a personal pride in the phrase: "Did ums." I did not even invent it. I found it, so to speak, when I got here, and my experience is that it soothes the Child. When he is howling, and I say "Did ums" with sympathetic intonation, he stops crying. Possibly enough it is astonishment at the ineptitude of the remark that silences him. Maybe it is that minor troubles are lost sight of face to face with the reflection that this is the sort of father with which fate has provided him. But may not even this be useful to him? He has got to meet with stupid people in the world. Let him begin by contemplating me. It will make things easier for him later on. I put forward the idea in the hope of comforting the young gentleman from Cambridge.

We injure the health of the Child by enforcing on it silence. We have a stupid formula that children should be seen and not heard. We deny it exercise to its lungs. We discourage its natural and laudable curiosity by telling it not to worry us— not to ask so many questions.

Won't somebody lend the young gentleman from Cambridge a small and healthy child just for a week or so, and let the bargain be that he lives with it all the time? The young gentleman from Cambridge thinks, when we call up the stairs to say that if we hear another sound from the nursery during the next two hours we will come up and do things to that Child the mere thought of which should appal it, that is silencing the Child. It does not occur to him that two minutes later that Child is yelling again at the top of its voice, having forgotten all we ever said.

[The Child of Fiction.]

I know the sort of Child the weeper over Children's wrongs has in his mind. It has deep, soulful, yearning eyes. It moves about the house softly, shedding an atmosphere of patient resignation. It says: "Yes, dear papa." "No, dear mamma." It has but one ambition—to be good and useful. It has beautiful thoughts about the stars. You don't know whether it is in the house or isn't: you find it with its little face pressed close against the window-pane watching the golden sunset. Nobody understands it. It blesses the old people and dies. One of these days the young gentleman from Cambridge will, one hopes, have a Baby of his own—a real Child: and serve him darn-well right.

Jerome K. Jerome

At present he is labouring under a wrong conception of the article. He says we over-educate it. We clog its wonderful brain with a mass of uninteresting facts and foolish formulas that we call knowledge. He does not know that all this time the Child is alive and kicking. He is under the delusion that the Child is taking all this lying down. We tell the Child it has got to be quiet, or else we will wring its neck. The gentleman from Cambridge pictures the Child as from that moment a silent spirit moving voiceless towards the grave.

We catch the Child in the morning, and clean it up, and put a little satchel on its back, and pack it off to school; and the maiden lady Understander pictures that Child wasting the all too brief period of youth crowding itself up with knowledge.

My dear Madam, you take it from me that your tears are being wasted. You wipe your eyes and cheer up. The dear Child is not going to be overworked: HE is seeing to that.

As a matter of the fact, the Child of the present day is having, if anything, too good a time. I shall be considered a brute for saying this, but I am thinking of its future, and my opinion is that we are giving it swelled head. The argument just now in the air is that the parent exists merely for the Children. The parent doesn't count. It is as if a gardener were to say,

"Bother the flowers, let them rot. The sooner they are out of the way the better. The seed is the only thing that interests me."

You can't produce respectable seed but from carefully cultivated flowers. The philosopher, clamouring for improved Children, will later grasp the fact that the parent is of importance. Then he will change his tactics, and address the Children, and we shall have our time. He will impress on them how necessary it is for their own sakes that they should be careful of us. We shall have books written about misunderstood fathers who were worried into early graves.

[The misunderstood Father.]

Fresh Air Funds will be started for sending parents away to the seaside on visits to kind bachelors living in detached houses, miles away from Children. Books will be specially written for us picturing a world where school fees are never demanded and babies never howl o' nights. Societies for the Prevention of Cruelty to Parents will arise. Little girls who get their hair entangled and mislay all their clothes just before they are starting for the party—little boys who kick holes in their best shoes will be spanked at the public expense.

Jerome K. Jerome

# CHAPTER XVIII

[Marriage and the Joke of it.]

Marriages are made in heaven—"but solely," it has been added by a cynical writer, "for export." There is nothing more remarkable in human sociology than our attitude towards the institution of marriage. So it came home to me the other evening as I sat on a cane chair in the ill-lighted schoolroom of a small country town. The occasion was a Penny Reading. We had listened to the usual overture from Zampa, played by the lady professor and the eldest daughter of the brewer; to "Phil Blood's Leap," recited by the curate; to the violin solo by the pretty widow about whom gossip is whispered—one hopes it is not true. Then a pale-faced gentleman, with a drooping black moustache, walked on to the platform. It was the local tenor. He sang to us a song of love. Misunderstandings had arisen; bitter words, regretted as soon as uttered, had pierced the all too sensitive spirit. Parting had followed. The broken-hearted one had died believing his affection unrequited. But the angels had since told him; he knew she loved him now—the accent on the now.

I glanced around me. We were the usual crowd of mixed humanity—tinkers, tailors, soldiers, sailors, with our cousins, and our sisters, and our wives. So many of our eyes were wet with tears. Miss Butcher could hardly repress her sobs. Young Mr. Tinker, his face hidden behind his programme, pretended to be blowing his nose. Mrs. Apothecary's large bosom heaved with heartfelt sighs. The retired Colonel sniffed audibly.

Sadness rested on our souls. It might have been so different but for those foolish, hasty words! There need have been no funeral. Instead, the church might have been decked with bridal flowers. How sweet she would have looked beneath her orange wreath! How proudly, gladly, he might have responded "I will," take her for his wedded wife, to have and to hold from this day forward, for better for worse, for richer for poorer, in sickness and in health, to love and to cherish, till death did them part. And thereto he might have plighted his troth.

In the silence which reigned after the applause had subsided the beautiful words of the Marriage Service seemed to be stealing through the room: that they might ever remain in perfect love and peace together. Thy wife shall be as the fruitful vine. Thy children like the olive branches round about thy table. Lo! thus shall a man be blessed. So shall men love their wives as their own bodies, and be not bitter against them, giving honour unto them as unto the weaker vessel. Let the wife see that she reverence her husband, wearing the ornament of a meek and quiet spirit.

[Love and the Satyr.]

All the stories sung by the sweet singers of all time were echoing in our ears—stories of true love that would not run smoothly until the last chapter; of gallant lovers strong and brave against fate; of tender sweethearts, waiting, trusting, till love's golden crown was won; so they married and lived happy ever after.

Then stepped briskly on the platform a stout, bald-headed man. We greeted him with enthusiasm—it was the local low comedian. The piano tinkled saucily. The self-confident man winked and opened wide his mouth. It was a funny song; how we roared with laughter! The last line of each verse was the same:

"And that's what it's like when you're married."

"Before it was 'duckie,' and 'darling,' and 'dear.' Now it's 'Take your cold feet away, Brute! can't you hear?'

"Once they walked hand in hand: 'Me loves ickle 'oo.' Now he strides on ahead" (imitation with aid of umbrella much appreciated; the bald-headed man, in his enthusiasm and owing to the smallness of the platform, sweeping the lady accompanist off her stool), "bawling: 'Come along, do.'"

The bald-headed man interspersed side-splitting patter. The husband comes home late; the wife is waiting for him at the top of the stairs with a broom. He kisses the servant-girl. She retaliates by discovering a cousin in the Guards.

The comic man retired to an enthusiastic demand for an encore. I looked around me at the laughing faces. Miss Butcher had been compelled to stuff her handkerchief into her mouth. Mr. Tinker was wiping his eyes; he was not ashamed this time, they were tears of merriment. Mrs. Apothecary's motherly bosom was shaking like a jelly. The Colonel was grinning from ear to ear.

Later on, as I noticed in the programme, the schoolmistress, an unmarried lady, was down to sing "Darby and Joan." She has a sympathetic voice. Her "Darby and Joan" is always popular. The comic man would also again appear in the second part, and would oblige with (by request) "His Mother-in-Law."

So the quaint comedy continues: To-night we will enjoy Romeo and Juliet, for to-morrow we have seats booked for The Pink Domino.

[What the Gipsy did not mention.]

"Won't the pretty lady let the poor old gipsy tell her fortune?" Blushes, giggles, protestations. Gallant gentleman friend insists. A dark man is in love with pretty lady. Gipsy sees a marriage not so very far ahead. Pretty lady says "What nonsense!" but looks serious. Pretty lady's pretty friends must, of course, be teasing. Gallant gentleman friend, by curious coincidence, happens to be dark. Gipsy grins and passes on.

Is that all the gipsy knows of pretty lady's future? The rheumy, cunning eyes! They were bonny and black many years ago, when the parchment skin was smooth and fair. They have seen so many a passing show—do they see in pretty lady's hand nothing further?

What would the wicked old eyes foresee did it pay them to speak: —Pretty lady crying tears into a pillow. Pretty lady growing ugly, spite and anger spoiling pretty features. Dark young man no longer loving. Dark young man hurling bitter words at pretty lady—hurling, maybe, things more heavy. Dark young man and pretty lady listening approvingly to comic singer, having both discovered: "That's what it's like when you're married."

My friend H. G. Wells wrote a book, "The Island of Dr. Moreau." I read it in MS. one winter evening in a lonely country house upon the hills, wind screaming to wind in the dark without. The story has haunted me ever since. I hear the wind's shrill laughter. The doctor had taken the beasts of the forest, apes, tigers, strange creatures from the deep, had fashioned them with hideous cruelty into the shapes of men, had given them souls, had taught to them the law. In all things else were they human, but their original instincts their creator's skill had failed to eliminate. All their lives were one long torture. The Law said, "We are men and women; this we shall do, this we shall not do." But the ape and tiger still cried aloud within them.

Civilization lays her laws upon us; they are the laws of gods—of the men that one day, perhaps, shall come. But the primeval creature of the cave still cries within us.

[A few rules for Married Happiness.]

The wonder is that not being gods—being mere men and

women—marriage works out as well as it does. We take two creatures with the instincts of the ape still stirring within them; two creatures fashioned on the law of selfishness; two self-centred creatures of opposite appetites, of desires opposed to one another, of differing moods and fancies; two creatures not yet taught the lesson of self- control, of self-renunciation, and bind them together for life in an union so close that one cannot snore o'nights without disturbing the other's rest; that one cannot, without risk to happiness, have a single taste unshared by the other; that neither, without danger of upsetting the whole applecart, so to speak, can have an opinion with which the other does not heartedly agree.

Could two angels exist together on such terms without ever quarrelling? I doubt it. To make marriage the ideal we love to picture it in romance, the elimination of human nature is the first essential. Supreme unselfishness, perfect patience, change-less amiability, we should have to start with, and continue with, until the end.

[The real Darby and Joan.]

I do not believe in the "Darby and Joan" of the song. They belong to song-land. To accept them I need a piano, a sympathetic contralto voice, a firelight effect, and that sentimental mood in myself, the foundation of which is a good dinner well digested. But there are Darbys and Joans of real flesh and blood to be met with—God bless them, and send more for our example—wholesome living men and women, brave, struggling, souls with common-sense. Ah, yes! they have quarrelled; had their dark house of bitterness, of hate, when he wished to heaven he had never met her, and told her so. How could he have guessed those sweet lips could utter such cruel words; those tender eyes, he loved to kiss, flash with scorn and anger?

And she, had she known what lay behind; those days when he knelt before her, swore that his only dream was to save her from all pain. Passion lies dead; it is a flame that burns out quickly. The most beautiful face in the world grows indifferent to us when we have sat opposite it every morning at breakfast, every evening at supper, for a brief year or two. Passion is the seed. Love grows from it, a tender sapling, beautiful to look upon, but wondrous frail, easily broken, easily trampled on during those first years of wedded life. Only by much nursing, by long caring-for, watered with tears, shall it grow into a sturdy tree, defiant of the winds, 'neath which Darby and Joan shall sit sheltered in old age.

They had commonsense, brave hearts. Darby had expected too much. Darby had not made allowance for human nature which he ought to have done, seeing how much he had of it himself. Joan knows he did not mean it. Joan has a nasty temper; she admits it. Joan will try, Darby will try. They kiss again with tears. It is a workaday world; Darby and Joan will take it as it is, will do their best. A little kindness, a little clasping of the hands before night comes.

[Many ways of Love]

Youth deems it heresy, but I sometimes wonder if our English speaking way is quite the best. I discussed the subject once with an old French lady. The English reader forms his idea of French life from the French novel; it leads to mistaken notions. There are French Darbys, French Joans, many thousands of them.

"Believe me," said my old French friend, "your English way is wrong; our way is not perfect, but it is the better, I am sure. You leave it entirely to the young people. What do they know of life, of themselves, even. He falls in love with a pretty face. She—he danced so well! he was so agreeable that day of the picnic! If marriage were only for a month or so; could be ended without harm when the passion was burnt out. Ah, yes! then perhaps you would be right. I loved at eighteen, madly— nearly broke my heart. I meet him occasionally now. My dear"—her hair was silvery white, and I was only thirty-five; she always called me "my dear"; it is pleasant at thirty-five to be talked to as a child. "He was a perfect brute, handsome he had been, yes, but all that was changed. He was as stupid as an ox. I never see his poor frightened-looking wife without shuddering thinking of what I have escaped. They told me all that, but I looked only at his face, and did not believe them. They forced me into marriage with the kindest man that ever lived. I did not love him then, but I loved him for thirty years; was it not better?"

"But, my dear friend," I answered; "that poor, frightened-looking wife of your first love! Her marriage also was, I take it, the result of parental choosing. The love marriage, I admit, as often as not turns out sadly. The children choose ill. Parents also choose ill. I fear there is no sure receipt for the happy marriage."

"You are arguing from bad examples," answered my silver-haired friend; "it is the system that I am defending. A young girl is no judge of character. She is easily deceived, is wishful to be deceived. As I have said, she does not even know herself. She imagines the mood of the moment will remain with her. Only those who have watched over her with loving insight from her infancy know her real temperament.

"The young man is blinded by his passion. Nature knows nothing of marriage, of companionship. She has only one aim. That accomplished, she is indifferent to the future of those she has joined together. I would have parents think only of their children's happiness, giving to worldly considerations their true value, but nothing beyond, choosing for their children with loving care, with sense of their great responsibility."

[Which is it?]

"I fear our young people would not be contented with our choosing," I suggested.

"Are they so contented with their own, the honeymoon over?" she responded with a smile.

We agreed it was a difficult problem viewed from any point.

But I still think it would be better were we to heap less ridicule upon the institution. Matrimony cannot be "holy" and ridiculous at the same time. We have been familiar with it long enough to make up our minds in which light to regard it.

Jerome K. Jerome

# CHAPTER XIX

[Man and his Tailor.]

What's wrong with the "Made-up Tie"? I gather from the fashionable novelist that no man can wear a made-up tie and be a gentleman. He may be a worthy man, clever, well-to-do, eligible from every other point of view; but She, the refined heroine, can never get over the fact that he wears a made-up tie. It causes a shudder down her high- bred spine whenever she thinks of it. There is nothing else to be said against him. There is nothing worse about him than this—he wears a made-up tie. It is all sufficient. No true woman could ever care for him, no really classy society ever open its doors to him.

I am worried about this thing because, to confess the horrid truth, I wear a made-up tie myself. On foggy afternoons I steal out of the house disguised. They ask me where I am going in a hat that comes down over my ears, and why I am wearing blue spectacles and a false beard, but I will not tell them. I creep along the wall till I find a common hosier's shop, and then, in an assumed voice, I tell the man what it is I want. They come to fourpence halfpenny each; by taking the half-dozen I get them for a trifle less. They are put on in a moment, and, to my vulgar eye, look neat and tasteful.

Of course, I know I am not a gentleman. I have given up hopes of ever being one. Years ago, when life presented possibilities, I thought that with pains and intelligence I might become one. I never succeeded. It all depends on being able to tie a bow. Round the bed-post, or the neck of the water-jug, I could tie the wretched thing to perfection. If only the bed-post or the water-jug could have taken my place and gone to the party instead of me, life would have been simpler. The bed-post and the water-jug, in its neat white bow, looked like a gentleman—the fashionable novelist's idea of a gentleman. Upon myself the result was otherwise, suggesting always a feeble attempt at suicide by strangulation. I could never understand how it was done. There were moments when it flashed across me that the secret lay in being able to turn one's self inside out, coming up with one's arms and legs the other way round. Standing on one's head might have surmounted the difficulty; but the higher gymnastics Nature has denied to me. "The Boneless Wonder" or the "Man Serpent" could, I felt, be a gentleman so easily. To one to whom has been given only the common ordinary joints gentlemanliness is apparently an impossible ideal.

It is not only the tie. I never read the fashionable novel without misgiving. Some hopeless bounder is being described:

"If you want to know what he is like," says the Peer of the Realm, throwing himself back in his deep easy-chair, and puffing lazily at his cigar of delicate aroma, "he is the sort of man that wears three studs in his shirt."

[The difficulty of being a Gentleman.]

Merciful heavens! I myself wear three studs in my shirt. I also am a hopeless bounder, and I never knew it. It comes upon me like a thunderbolt. I thought three studs were fashionable. The idiot at the shop told me three studs were all the rage, and I ordered two dozen. I can't afford to throw them away. Till these two dozen shirts are worn out, I shall have to remain a hopeless bounder.

Why have we not a Minister of the Fine Arts? Why does not a paternal Government fix notices at the street corners, telling the would-be gentleman how many studs he ought to wear, what style of necktie now distinguishes the noble-minded man from the base-hearted? They are prompt enough with their police regulations, their vaccination orders—the higher things of life they neglect.

I select at random another masterpiece of English literature.

"My dear," says Lady Montresor, with her light aristocratic laugh, "you surely cannot seriously think of marrying a man who wears socks with yellow spots?"

Lady Emmelina sighs.

"He is very nice," she murmurs, "but I suppose you are right. I suppose that sort of man does get on your nerves after a time."

"My dear child," says Lady Montresor, "he is impossible."

In a cold sweat I rush upstairs into my bedroom.

I thought so: I am always wrong. All my best socks have yellow spots. I rather fancied them. They were expensive, too, now I come to think of it.

What am I to do? If I sacrifice them and get red spots, then red spots, for all I know, may be wrong. I have no instinct. The fashionable novelist never helps one. He tells us what is wrong, but he does not tell us what is right. It is creative criticism that I feel the need of. Why does not the Lady Montresor go on? Tell me what sort of socks the ideal lover ought to wear. There are so many varieties of socks. What is a would-be-gentleman to do? Would it be of any use writing to the fashionable novelist:-

[How we might, all of us, be Gentlemen.]

"Dear Mr. Fashionable Novelist (or should it be Miss?), —Before going to my tailor, I venture to write to you on a subject of some importance. I am fairly well educated, of good family and address, and, so my friends tell me, of passable appearance. I yearn to become a gentleman. If it is not troubling you too much, would you mind telling me how to set about the business? What socks and ties ought I to wear? Do I wear a flower in my button-hole, or is that a sign of a coarse mind? How many buttons on a morning coat show a beautiful nature? Does a stand-up collar with a tennis shirt prove that you are of noble descent, or, on the contrary, stamp you as a parvenu? If answering these questions imposes too great a tax on your time, perhaps you would not mind telling me how you yourself know these things. Who is your authority, and when is he at home? I should apologize for writing to you but that I feel you will sympathize with my appeal. It seems a pity there should be so many vulgar, ill-bred people in the world when a little knowledge on these trivial points would enable us all to become gentlemen. Thanking you in anticipation, I remain . . . "

Would he or she tell us? Or would the fashionable novelist reply as I once overheard a harassed mother retort upon one of her inquiring children. Most of the afternoon she had been rushing out into the garden, where games were in progress, to tell the children what they must not do: —"Tommy, you know you must not do that. Haven't you got any sense at all?" "Johnny, you wicked boy, how dare you do that; how many more times do you want me to tell you?" "Jane, if you do that again you will go straight to bed, my girl!" and so on.

At length the door was opened from without, and a little face peeped in: "Mother!"

"Now, what is it? can't I ever get a moment's peace?"

"Mother, please would you mind telling us something we might do?"

The lady almost fell back on the floor in her astonishment. The idea had never occurred to her.

Jerome K. Jerome

"What may you do! Don't ask me. I am tired enough of telling you what not to do."

[Things a Gentleman should never do.]

I remember when a young man, wishful to conform to the rules of good society, I bought a book of etiquette for gentlemen. Its fault was just this. It told me through many pages what not to do. Beyond that it seemed to have no idea. I made a list of things it said a gentleman should NEVER do: it was a lengthy list.

Determined to do the job completely while I was about it, I bought other books of etiquette and added on their list of "Nevers." What one book left out another supplied. There did not seem much left for a gentleman to do.

I concluded by the time I had come to the end of my books, that to be a true gentleman my safest course would be to stop in bed for the rest of my life. By this means only could I hope to avoid every possible faux pas, every solecism. I should have lived and died a gentleman. I could have had it engraved upon my tombstone:

"He never in his life committed a single act unbecoming to a gentleman."

To be a gentleman is not so easy, perhaps, as a fashionable novelist imagines. One is forced to the conclusion that it is not a question entirely for the outfitter. My attention was attracted once by a notice in the window of a West-End emporium, "Gentlemen supplied."

It is to such like Universal Providers that the fashionable novelist goes for his gentleman. The gentleman is supplied to him complete in every detail. If the reader be not satisfied, that is the reader's fault. He is one of those tiresome, discontented customers who does not know a good article when he has got it.

I was told the other day of the writer of a musical farce (or is it comedy?) who was most desirous that his leading character should be a perfect gentleman. During the dress rehearsal, the actor representing the part had to open his cigarette case and request another perfect gentleman to help himself. The actor drew forth his case. It caught the critical eye of the author.

"Good heavens!" he cried, "what do you call that?"

"A cigarette case," answered the actor.

"But, my dear boy," exclaimed the author, "surely it is silver?"

"I know," admitted the actor, "it does perhaps suggest that I am living beyond my means, but the truth is I picked it up cheap."

The author turned to the manager.

"This won't do," he explained, "a real gentleman always carries a gold cigarette case. He must be a gentleman, or there's no point in the plot."

"Don't let us endanger any point the plot may happen to possess, for goodness sake," agreed the manager, "let him by all means have a gold cigarette case."

[How one may know the perfect Gentleman.]

So, regardless of expense, a gold cigarette case was obtained and put down to expenses. And yet on the first night of that musical play, when that leading personage smashed a tray over a waiter's head, and, after a row with the police, came home drunk to his wife, even that gold cigarette case failed to convince one that the man was a gentleman beyond all doubt.

The old writers appear to have been singularly unaware of the importance attaching to these socks, and ties, and cigarette-cases. They told us merely what the man felt and thought.

What reliance can we place upon them? How could they possibly have known what sort of man he was underneath his clothes? Tweed or broadcloth is not transparent. Even could they have got rid of his clothes there would have remained his flesh and bones. It was pure guess-work. They did not observe.

The modern writer goes to work scientifically. He tells us that the creature wore a made-up tie. From that we know he was not a gentleman; it follows as the night the day. The fashionable novelist notices the young man's socks. It reveals to us whether the marriage would have been successful or a failure. It is necessary to convince us that the hero is a perfect gentleman: the author gives him a gold cigarette case.

A well-known dramatist has left it on record that comedy cannot exist nowadays, for the simple reason that gentlemen have given up taking snuff and wearing swords. How can one have comedy in company with frock-coats—without its "Las" and its "Odds Bobs."

The sword may have been helpful. I have been told that at levees City men, unaccustomed to the thing, have, with its help, provided comedy for the rest of the company.

But I take it this is not the comedy our dramatist had in mind.

[Why not an Exhibition of Gentlemen?]

It seems a pity that comedy should disappear from among us. If it depend entirely on swords and snuff-boxes, would it not be worth the while of the Society of Authors to keep a few gentlemen specially trained? Maybe some sympathetic theatrical manager would lend us costumes of the eighteenth century. We might provide them with swords and snuff-boxes. They might meet, say, once a week, in a Queen Anne drawing-room, especially prepared by Gillow, and go through their tricks. Authors seeking high-class comedy might be admitted to a gallery.

Perhaps this explains why old-fashioned readers complain that we do not give them human nature. How can we? Ladies and gentlemen nowadays don't wear the proper clothes. Evidently it all depends upon the clothes.

Jerome K. Jerome

# CHAPTER XX

[Woman and her behaviour.]

Should women smoke?

The question, in four-inch letters, exhibited on a placard outside a small newsvendor's shop, caught recently my eye. The wanderer through London streets is familiar with such-like appeals to his decision: "Should short men marry tall wives?" "Ought we to cut our hair?" "Should second cousins kiss?" Life's problems appear to be endless.

Personally, I am not worrying myself whether women should smoke or not. It seems to me a question for the individual woman to decide for herself. I like women who smoke; I can see no objection to their smoking. Smoking soothes the nerves. Women's nerves occasionally want soothing. The tiresome idiot who argues that smoking is unwomanly denounces the drinking of tea as unmanly. He is a wooden- headed person who derives all his ideas from cheap fiction. The manly man of cheap fiction smokes a pipe and drinks whisky. That is how we know he is a man. The womanly woman—well, I always feel I could make a better woman myself out of an old clothes shop and a hair-dresser's block.

But, as I have said, the question does not impress me as one demanding my particular attention. I also like the woman who does not smoke. I have met in my time some very charming women who do not smoke. It may be a sign of degeneracy, but

I am prepared to abdicate my position of woman's god, leaving her free to lead her own life.

[Woman's God.]

Candidly, the responsibility of feeling myself answerable for all a woman does or does not do would weigh upon me. There are men who are willing to take this burden upon themselves, and a large number of women are still anxious that they should continue to bear it. I spoke quite seriously to a young lady not long ago on the subject of tight lacing; undoubtedly she was injuring her health. She admitted it herself.

"I know all you can say," she wailed; "I daresay a lot of it is true. Those awful pictures where one sees—well, all the things one does not want to think about. If they are correct, it must be bad, squeezing it all up together."

"Then why continue to do so?" I argued.

"Oh, it's easy enough to talk," she explained; "a few old fogies like you"—I had been speaking very plainly to her, and she was cross with me—"may pretend you don't like small waists, but the average man does."

Poor girl! She was quite prepared to injure herself for life, to damage her children's future, to be uncomfortable for fifteen hours a day, all to oblige the average man.

It is a compliment to our sex. What man would suffer injury and torture to please the average woman? This frenzied desire of woman to conform to our ideals is touching. A few daring spirits of late years have exhibited a tendency to seek for other gods—for ideals of their own. We call them the unsexed women. The womanly women lift up their hands in horror of such blasphemy.

When I was a boy no womanly woman rode a bicycle—tricycles were permitted. On three wheels you could still be womanly, but on two you were "a creature"! The womanly woman, seeing her approach, would draw down the parlour blind with a jerk, lest the children looking out might catch a glimpse of her, and their young souls be smirched for all eternity.

No womanly woman rode inside a hansom or outside a 'bus. I remember the day my own dear mother climbed outside a 'bus for the first time in her life. She was excited, and cried a little; but nobody—heaven be praised!—saw us—that is, nobody of importance. And afterwards she confessed the air was pleasant.

"Be not the first by whom the new is tried, Nor yet the last to lay the old aside," is a safe rule for those who would always retain the good opinion of that all-powerful, but somewhat unintelligent, incubus, "the average person," but the pioneer, the guide, is necessary. That is, if the world is to move forward.

The freedom-loving girl of to-day, who can enjoy a walk by herself without losing her reputation, who can ride down the street on her "bike" without being hooted at, who can play a mixed double at tennis without being compelled by public opinion to marry her partner, who can, in short, lead a human creature's life, and not that of a lap- dog led about at the end of a string, might pause to think what she owes to the "unsexed creatures" who fought her battle for her fifty years ago.

[Those unsexed Creatures]

Can the working woman of to-day, who may earn her own living, if she will, without loss of the elementary rights of womanhood, think of the bachelor girl of a short generation ago without admiration of her pluck? There were ladies in those day too "unwomanly" to remain helpless burdens on overworked fathers and mothers, too "unsexed" to marry the first man that came along for the sake of their bread and butter. They fought their way into journalism, into the office, into the shop. The reformer is not always the pleasantest man to invite to a tea-party. Maybe these women who went forward with the flag were not the most charming of their sex. The "Dora Copperfield" type will for some time remain the young man's ideal, the model the young girl puts before herself. Myself, I think Dora Copperfield charming, but a world of Dora Copperfields!

The working woman is a new development in sociology. She has many lessons to learn, but one has hopes of her. It is said that she is unfitting herself to be a wife and mother. If the ideal helpmeet for a man be an animated Dresden china shepherdess —something that looks pretty on the table, something to be shown round to one's friends, something that can be locked up safely in a cupboard, that asks no questions, and, therefore, need be told no lies—then a woman who has learnt something of the world, who has formed ideas of her own, will not be the ideal wife.

[References given—and required.]

Maybe the average man will not be her ideal husband. Each Michaelmas at a little town in the Thames Valley with which I am acquainted there is held a hiring fair. A farmer one year laid his hand on a lively-looking lad, and asked him if he wanted a job. It was what the boy was looking for.

"Got a character?" asked the farmer. The boy replied that he had for the last two years been working for Mr. Muggs, the ironmonger—felt sure that Mr. Muggs would give him a good character.

"Well, go and ask Mr. Muggs to come across and speak to me, I will wait here," directed the would-be employer. Five minutes went by—ten minutes. No Mr. Muggs appeared. Later in the afternoon the farmer met the boy again.

"Mr. Muggs never came near me with that character of yours," said the farmer.

"No, sir," answered the boy, "I didn't ask him to."

"Why not?" inquired the farmer.

"Well, I told him who it was that wanted it"—the boy hesitated.

"Well?" demanded the farmer, impatiently.

"Well, then, he told me yours," explained the boy.

Maybe the working woman, looking for a husband, and not merely a livelihood, may end by formulating standards of her own. She may end by demanding the manly man and moving about the world, knowing something of life, may arrive at the conclusion that something more is needed than the smoking of pipes and the drinking of whiskies and sodas. We must be prepared for this. The sheltered woman who learnt her life from fairy stories is a dream of the past. Woman has escaped from her "shelter"—she is on the loose. For the future we men have got to accept the emancipated woman as an accomplished fact.

[The ideal World.]

Many of us are worried about her. What is going to become of the home? I admit there is a more ideal existence where the working woman would find no place; it is in a world that exists only on the comic opera stage. There every picturesque village contains an equal number of ladies and gentlemen nearly all the same height and weight, to all appearance of the same age. Each Jack has his Jill, and does not want anybody else's. There are no complications: one presumes they draw lots and fall in love the moment they unscrew the paper. They dance for awhile on grass which is never damp, and then into the conveniently situated ivy-covered church they troop in pairs and are wedded off hand by a white-haired clergyman, who is a married man himself.

Ah, if the world were but a comic opera stage, there would be no need for working women! As a matter of fact, so far as one can judge from the front of the house, there are no working men either.

But outside the opera house in the muddy street Jack goes home to his third floor back, or his chambers in the Albany, according to his caste, and wonders when the time will come when he will be able to support a wife. And Jill climbs on a penny 'bus, or steps into the family brougham, and dreams with regret of a lost garden, where there was just one man and just one woman, and clothes grew on a fig tree.

With the progress of civilization—utterly opposed as it is to all Nature's intentions—the number of working women will increase. With some friends the other day I was discussing motor-cars, and one gentleman with sorrow in his voice—he is the type of Conservative who would have regretted the passing away of the glacial period— opined that motor-cars had come to stay.

"You mean," said another, "they have come to go." The working woman, however much we may regret it, has come to go, and she is going it. We shall have to accept her and see what can be done with her. One thing is certain, we shall not solve the problem of the twentieth century by regretting the simple sociology of the Stone Age.

[A Lover's View.]

Speaking as a lover, I welcome the openings that are being given to women to earn their own livelihood. I can conceive of no more degrading profession for a woman—no profession more calculated to unfit her for being that wife and mother we talk so much about than the profession that up to a few years ago was the only one open to her—the profession of husband-hunting.

As a man, I object to being regarded as woman's last refuge, her one and only alternative to the workhouse. I cannot myself see why the woman who has faced the difficulties of existence, learnt the lesson of life, should not make as good a wife and mother as the ignorant girl taken direct, one might almost say, from the nursery, and, without the slightest preparation, put in a position of responsibility that to a thinking person must be almost appalling.

It has been said that the difference between men and women is this: That the man goes about the world making it ready for the children, that the woman stops at home making the children ready for the world. Will not she do it much better for knowing something of the world, for knowing something of the temptations, the difficulties, her own children will have to face, for having learnt by her own experience to sympathize with the struggles, the sordid heart-breaking cares that man has daily to contend with?

Civilization is ever undergoing transformation, but human nature remains. The bachelor girl, in her bed-sitting room, in her studio, in her flat, will still see in the shadows the vision of the home, will still hear in the silence the sound of children's voices, will still dream of the lover's kiss that is to open up new life to her. She is not quite so unsexed as you may think, my dear womanly madame. A male friend of mine was telling me of a catastrophe that once occurred at a station in the East Indies.

[No time to think of Husbands.]

A fire broke out at night, and everybody was in terror lest it should reach the magazine. The women and children were being hurried to the ships, and two ladies were hastening past my friend. One of them paused, and, clasping her hands, demanded of him if he knew what had become of her husband. Her companion was indignant.

"For goodness' sake, don't dawdle, Maria," she cried; "this is no time to think of husbands."

There is no reason to fear that the working woman will ever cease to think of husbands. Maybe, as I have said, she will demand a better article than the mere husband-hunter has been able to stand out for. Maybe she herself will have something more to give; maybe she will bring to him broader sympathies, higher ideals. The woman who has herself been down among the people, who has faced life in the open, will know that the home is but one cell of the vast hive.

We shall, perhaps, hear less of the woman who "has her own home and children to think of—really takes no interest in these matters"—these matters of right and wrong, these matters that spell the happiness or misery of millions.

[The Wife of the Future.]

Maybe the bridegroom of the future will not say, "I have married a wife, and therefore I cannot come," but "I have married a wife; we will both come."

Jerome K. Jerome

# ABOUT THE AUTHOR

 **Jerome Klapka Jerome** (May 2, 1859–June 14, 1927) was an English author, best known for the humorous travelogue Three Men in a Boat. Other works include the essay collections Idle Thoughts of an Idle Fellow and Second Thoughts of an Idle Fellow; Three Men on the Bummel, a sequel to Three Men in a Boat; and several other novels.

He was born at 1 Caldmore Road, on the corner of Bradford Street in Walsall, then in Staffordshire), where there is now a museum in his honour, and was brought up in poverty in London.

In 1898, a short stay in Germany inspired Three Men on the Bummel, the sequel to Three Men in a Boat. While reintroducing the same characters in the setting of a foreign bicycle tour, the book was nonetheless unable to capture the life-force and historic roots of its predecessor, and the book enjoyed only a mild success.

In 1926, Jerome published his autobiography My Life and Times. Shortly afterwards, the Borough of Walsall conferred on him the title, Freeman of the Borough.

# Choose from Thousands of 1stWorldLibrary Classics By

A. M. Barnard
Ada Leverson
Adolphus William Ward
Aesop
Agatha Christie
Alexander Aaronsohn
Alexander Kielland
Alexandre Dumas
Alfred Gatty
Alfred Ollivant
Alice Duer Miller
Alice Turner Curtis
Alice Dunbar
Allen Chapman
Alleyne Ireland
Ambrose Bierce
Amelia E. Barr
Amory H. Bradford
Andrew Lang
Andrew McFarland Davis
Andy Adams
Angela Brazil
Anna Alice Chapin
Anna Sewell
Annie Besant
Annie Hamilton Donnell
Annie Payson Call
Annie Roe Carr
Annonaymous
Anton Chekhov
Archibald Lee Fletcher
Arnold Bennett
Arthur C. Benson
Arthur Conan Doyle
Arthur M. Winfield
Arthur Ransome
Arthur Schnitzler
Arthur Train
Atticus
B.H. Baden-Powell
B. M. Bower
B. C. Chatterjee
Baroness Emmuska Orczy
Baroness Orczy
Basil King
Bayard Taylor
Ben Macomber
Bertha Muzzy Bower
Bjornstjerne Bjornson

Booth Tarkington
Boyd Cable
Bram Stoker
C. Collodi
C. E. Orr
C. M. Ingleby
Carolyn Wells
Catherine Parr Traill
Charles A. Eastman
Charles Amory Beach
Charles Dickens
Charles Dudley Warner
Charles Farrar Browne
Charles Ives
Charles Kingsley
Charles Klein
Charles Hanson Towne
Charles Lathrop Pack
Charles Romyn Dake
Charles Whibley
Charles Willing Beale
Charlotte M. Braeme
Charlotte M. Yonge
Charlotte Perkins Stetson
Clair W. Hayes
Clarence Day Jr.
Clarence E. Mulford
Clemence Housman
Confucius
Coningsby Dawson
Cornelis DeWitt Wilcox
Cyril Burleigh
D. H. Lawrence
Daniel Defoe
David Garnett
Dinah Craik
Don Carlos Janes
Donald Keyhoe
Dorothy Kilner
Dougan Clark
Douglas Fairbanks
E. Nesbit
E. P. Roe
E. Phillips Oppenheim
E. S. Brooks
Earl Barnes
Edgar Rice Burroughs
Edith Van Dyne
Edith Wharton

Edward Everett Hale
Edward J. O'Biren
Edward S. Ellis
Edwin L. Arnold
Eleanor Atkins
Eleanor Hallowell Abbott
Eliot Gregory
Elizabeth Gaskell
Elizabeth McCracken
Elizabeth Von Arnim
Ellem Key
Emerson Hough
Emilie F. Carlen
Emily Bronte
Emily Dickinson
Enid Bagnold
Enilor Macartney Lane
Erasmus W. Jones
Ernie Howard Pie
Ethel May Dell
Ethel Turner
Ethel Watts Mumford
Eugene Sue
Eugenie Foa
Eugene Wood
Eustace Hale Ball
Evelyn Everett-green
Everard Cotes
F. H. Cheley
F. J. Cross
F. Marion Crawford
Fannie E. Newberry
Federick Austin Ogg
Ferdinand Ossendowski
Fergus Hume
Florence A. Kilpatrick
Fremont B. Deering
Francis Bacon
Francis Darwin
Frances Hodgson Burnett
Frances Parkinson Keyes
Frank Gee Patchin
Frank Harris
Frank Jewett Mather
Frank L. Packard
Frank V. Webster
Frederic Stewart Isham
Frederick Trevor Hill
Frederick Winslow Taylor

Friedrich Kerst
Friedrich Nietzsche
Fyodor Dostoyevsky
G.A. Henty
G.K. Chesterton
Gabrielle E. Jackson
Garrett P. Serviss
Gaston Leroux
George A. Warren
George Ade
Geroge Bernard Shaw
George Cary Eggleston
George Durston
George Ebers
George Eliot
George Gissing
George MacDonald
George Meredith
George Orwell
George Sylvester Viereck
George Tucker
George W. Cable
George Wharton James
Gertrude Atherton
Gordon Casserly
Grace E. King
Grace Gallatin
Grace Greenwood
Grant Allen
Guillermo A. Sherwell
Gulielma Zollinger
Gustav Flaubert
H. A. Cody
H. B. Irving
H.C. Bailey
H. G. Wells
H. H. Munro
H. Irving Hancock
H. R. Naylor
H. Rider Haggard
H. W. C. Davis
Haldeman Julius
Hall Caine
Hamilton Wright Mabie
Hans Christian Andersen
Harold Avery
Harold McGrath
Harriet Beecher Stowe
Harry Castlemon
Harry Coghill
Harry Houidini

Hayden Carruth
Helent Hunt Jackson
Helen Nicolay
Hendrik Conscience
Hendy David Thoreau
Henri Barbusse
Henrik Ibsen
Henry Adams
Henry Ford
Henry Frost
Henry James
Henry Jones Ford
Henry Seton Merriman
Henry W Longfellow
Herbert A. Giles
Herbert Carter
Herbert N. Casson
Herman Hesse
Hildegard G. Frey
Homer
Honore De Balzac
Horace B. Day
Horace Walpole
Horatio Alger Jr.
Howard Pyle
Howard R. Garis
Hugh Lofting
Hugh Walpole
Humphry Ward
Ian Maclaren
Inez Haynes Gillmore
Irving Bacheller
Isabel Cecilia Williams
Isabel Hornibrook
Israel Abrahams
Ivan Turgenev
J.G.Austin
J. Henri Fabre
J. M. Barrie
J. M. Walsh
J. Macdonald Oxley
J. R. Miller
J. S. Fletcher
J. S. Knowles
J. Storer Clouston
J. W. Duffield
Jack London
Jacob Abbott
James Allen
James Andrews
James Baldwin

James Branch Cabell
James DeMille
James Joyce
James Lane Allen
James Lane Allen
James Oliver Curwood
James Oppenheim
James Otis
James R. Driscoll
Jane Abbott
Jane Austen
Jane L. Stewart
Janet Aldridge
Jens Peter Jacobsen
Jerome K. Jerome
Jessie Graham Flower
John Buchan
John Burroughs
John Cournos
John F. Kennedy
John Gay
John Glasworthy
John Habberton
John Joy Bell
John Kendrick Bangs
John Milton
John Philip Sousa
John Taintor Foote
Jonas Lauritz Idemil Lie
Jonathan Swift
Joseph A. Altsheler
Joseph Carey
Joseph Conrad
Joseph E. Badger Jr
Joseph Hergesheimer
Joseph Jacobs
Jules Vernes
Julian Hawthrone
Julie A Lippmann
Justin Huntly McCarthy
Kakuzo Okakura
Karle Wilson Baker
Kate Chopin
Kenneth Grahame
Kenneth McGaffey
Kate Langley Bosher
Kate Langley Bosher
Katherine Cecil Thurston
Katherine Stokes
L. A. Abbot
L. T. Meade

L. Frank Baum
Latta Griswold
Laura Dent Crane
Laura Lee Hope
Laurence Housman
Lawrence Beasley
Leo Tolstoy
Leonid Andreyev
Lewis Carroll
Lewis Sperry Chafer
Lilian Bell
. Lloyd Osbourne
Louis Hughes
Louis Joseph Vance
Louis Tracy
Louisa May Alcott
Lucy Fitch Perkins
Lucy Maud Montgomery
Luther Benson
Lydia Miller Middleton
Lyndon Orr
M. Corvus
M. H. Adams
Margaret E. Sangster
Margret Howth
Margaret Vandercook
Margaret W. Hungerford
Margret Penrose
Maria Edgeworth
Maria Thompson Daviess
Mariano Azuela
Marion Polk Angellotti
Mark Overton
Mark Twain
Mary Austin
Mary Catherine Crowley
Mary Cole
Mary Hastings Bradley
Mary Roberts Rinehart
Mary Rowlandson
M. Wollstonecraft Shelley
Maud Lindsay
Max Beerbohm
Myra Kelly
Nathaniel Hawthrone
Nicolo Machiavelli
O. F. Walton
Oscar Wilde

Owen Johnson
P.G. Wodehouse
Paul and Mabel Thorne
Paul G. Tomlinson
Paul Severing
Percy Brebner
Percy Keese Fitzhugh
Peter B. Kyne
Plato
Quincy Allen
R. Derby Holmes
R. L. Stevenson
R. S. Ball
Rabindranath Tagore
Rahul Alvares
Ralph Bonehill
Ralph Henry Barbour
Ralph Victor
Ralph Waldo Emmerson
Rene Descartes
Ray Cummings
Rex Beach
Rex E. Beach
Richard Harding Davis
Richard Jefferies
Richard Le Gallienne
Robert Barr
Robert Frost
Robert Gordon Anderson
Robert L. Drake
Robert Lansing
Robert Lynd
Robert Michael Ballantyne
Robert W. Chambers
Rosa Nouchette Carey
Rudyard Kipling
Saint Augustine
Samuel B. Allison
Samuel Hopkins Adams
Sarah Bernhardt
Sarah C. Hallowell
Selma Lagerlof
Sherwood Anderson
Sigmund Freud
Standish O'Grady
Stanley Weyman
Stella Benson
Stella M. Francis

Stephen Crane
Stewart Edward White
Stijn Streuvels
Swami Abhedananda
Swami Parmananda
T. S. Ackland
T. S. Arthur
The Princess Der Ling
Thomas A. Janvier
Thomas A Kempis
Thomas Anderton
Thomas Bailey Aldrich
Thomas Bulfinch
Thomas De Quincey
Thomas Dixon
Thomas H. Huxley
Thomas Hardy
Thomas More
Thornton W. Burgess
U. S. Grant
Upton Sinclair
Valentine Williams
Various Authors
Vaughan Kester
Victor Appleton
Victor G. Durham
Victoria Cross
Virginia Woolf
Wadsworth Camp
Walter Camp
Walter Scott
Washington Irving
Wilbur Lawton
Wilkie Collins
Willa Cather
Willard F. Baker
William Dean Howells
William le Queux
W. Makepeace Thackeray
William W. Walter
William Shakespeare
Winston Churchill
Yei Theodora Ozaki
Yogi Ramacharaka
Young E. Allison
Zane Grey

www.ingramcontent.com/pod-product-compliance
Lightning Source LLC
Chambersburg PA
CBHW051830170626
46807CB00003B/1102